BEADS
BUTTONS
& BOWS

BEADS
BUTTONS
& BOWS

Grange
BOOKS

A QUANTUM BOOK

Published by Grange Books
An imprint of Grange Books plc
The Grange
Grange Yard
London SE1 3AG

ISBN 1-84013-064-4

QUMBUB

This book was designed and produced by
Quantum Books Ltd
6 Blundell Street
London N7 9BH

Printed in China by Leefung-Asco Printers Ltd

CONTENTS

MATERIALS

Most of the projects in this book require very little in the way of specialist materials and equipment, although there are a few basic items that you will need. You may well already have these in your sewing or household tool box, but, if not, they are inexpensive to buy and readily available from the local shopping centre, from specialist craft outlets and by mail order.

Having the correct equipment at hand will make working the projects much easier and will also give a professional finish, so it is worth investing in the right tools before you start. Shown here are the basic items you will need.

PLIERS

Small jeweller's pliers with fine, smooth tips are needed for shaping jewellery findings. If these do not have a cutting edge, wire-cutters will also be needed.

FINDINGS

Findings are the metal components used for jewellery, and are usually made from a base metal plated with a silver, gold or nickel solution.

1 Jump rings link various jewellery components and findings. **2** Triangle bails are used to hang thicker beads, which will not take a jump ring. **3** Eye pins are threaded through beads to link them together and to other findings. **4** Head pins are used in the same way as eye pins.

5 Screw clasps consist of two halves which screw together. **6** Pierced-ear wires come in various shapes. **7** Bell caps conceal multi-strand thread ends on a necklace or earrings. **8** Brooch backs provide a base for sewn or glued beads. **9** Posts with butterfly fastenings for pierced ears. **10** Decorative clasps secure the ends of necklaces and bracelets. **11** Screw and clip fastenings for non-pierced ears.

THREADS

Your choice of thread will depend on the size of bead and the effect required. **1** Stranded silk is ideal for fine work. **2** Metallic and iridescent threads add texture and interest. **3** Cotton threads can be chosen to match a colour scheme. **4** Use thicker thread when strength is needed.

NEEDLES

You will need various types of needle for bead work.
1 Fine, pliable beading needles and fine quilting needles are both extremely useful. **2** Leather needles are strong with sharp, angled points. **3** Curved needles are invaluable for stitching beads to awkward shapes.

BRADAWL

A bradawl is used for starting a hole in leather or hide prior to stitching on beads with a needle.

FUSIBLE INTERFACING

Fusible interfacing is used as a base for ribbon weaving – ribbons can be fused to one side of the interfacing and held in position to form a "fabric." Interfacing is available in light, medium, and heavy weights.

GLUES

Your choice of adhesive will depend on the materials you are using. Check the instructions before application. **1** Two-part epoxy glue is very strong and usually dries to a clear finish. **2** A good, general-purpose PVA-based craft glue will suffice for most projects.

SCISSORS

Good scissors are essential for working with beads. **1** Use sharp-pointed embroidery scissors for snipping thread ends. **2** General-purpose craft scissors.

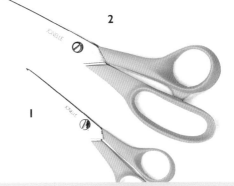

BEADS

Beads have featured in jewellery design and decorative art for well over five thousand years, and have always been highly prized. They have been worn as symbols to display both power and wealth, traded for gold, ivory and even slaves, and in some cultures used to ward off evil. The history of beads has often mirrored social, economic and even political events through the centuries, and is certainly worth studying if you have the chance.

Beads are available today in a wonderful array of shapes and sizes, and come in such a kaleidoscopic range of colours, with transparent, opaque, metallic, iridescent and natural finishes, that they are one of the most exciting materials with which to work. The major bead "types" are shown here.

GLASS BEADS

Tiny glass beads, often used in decorative embroidery, are known as rocailles or seed beads. Tube-shaped bugle beads are perfect for embroidery and bead fringes. Larger coloured-glass beads are ideal for jewellery, and, if faceted, reflect the light superbly, making them ideal for tassels and fringes.

PLASTIC BEADS

Plastic beads can be moulded and faceted to resemble glass, and are much lighter and less expensive than the real thing. They can also have a metallic finish.

METAL BEADS

Metal beads with gold, silver or bronze finishes are very useful. They range from bright, shiny, modern beads in irregular shapes to beautiful antique-style beads with inset decoration. Metal beads create rich effects for jewellery or accessories.

WOODEN BEADS

Wooden beads give a natural feel to clothing and jewellery. They may be plain, highly polished to show off the natural grain, carved, or painted with bright primary colours.

CERAMIC BEADS

Ceramic beads, made from fired clay, are often exquisitely decorated and are perfect for colourful jewellery. Synthetic clays can also be used to give a similar effect. Stone beads often have a beautiful glazed finish.

EMBROIDERY STONES

Flat-backed "jewel" beads are ideal for use on practical items such as bags or cushions, as they will not catch on other objects. They usually have small holes on either side for attaching to fabric, but can also have a single central hole.

NATURAL BEADS

Carved or smooth bone beads have a lovely texture and look wonderful on clothing and for chunky jewellery. Plastic imitations are available if you prefer, and make a cheaper alternative. The iridescent quality of synthetic-pearl beads makes a beautiful decoration on almost any surface.

SEQUINS

Although not technically beads, bright metallic and iridescent sequins are often used alongside beads to add detail and texture.

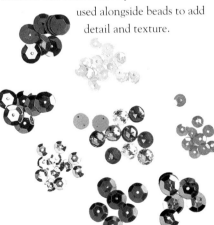

NOVELTY BEADS

Colourful novelty beads make fun pieces of jewellery or decoration on children's clothes or accessories.

BEAD TECHNIQUES

Each of the projects in this book has its own set of instructions, but there are some basic techniques for working with beads that are useful to know. These will enable you to add a professional finish to your work, and will make the difference between items that feel "home-made" and pieces of work that look expensive and shop-bought.

HOW TO WORK KNOTS

Knotting between the beads gives an authentic Victorian look to necklaces and bracelets, and using a colourful silk or textured thread will also enhance the look of the beads. It is important that the knots you make are large enough not to slip into the bead holes, so use several strands of thread if necessary.

A basic knot will be adequate for most purposes. For a knotted necklace or bracelet, begin with a knot, thread on a bead and loosely form the next knot, using

a needle to draw it up close to the bead. Continue in this way, making the knots as even as possible, finish with a knot and work the thread ends back through the beads to conceal them. Add a finding to each end to complete the necklace or bracelet.

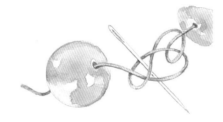

If you require a more secure knot, take the thread through the loop of the knot twice, and use a needle to pull it up close to a bead or finding.

A figure-of-eight knot gives a solid finish and is useful when securing thread ends inside a calotte.

EMBROIDERING BEADS INDIVIDUALLY

Applying a lot of beads individually to fabric requires patience, but is well worth the effort. Fabric is the easiest surface for this, but you can also apply beads to leather with the help of a bradawl (see page 9).

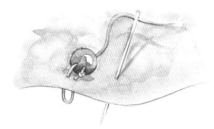

For rocailles, seed beads and round beads, use a fine beading needle and either matching or invisible thread. Tie a knot in one end of the thread, take the needle through from the right side and make two or three tiny stitches on the wrong side (the knot will be concealed by the first bead). Take the needle through to the right side again and thread on the first bead, bringing the needle back through to the wrong side close to the end of the bead, so that it lies firmly in place.

Make a back stitch every third bead or so to give the work a secure finish.

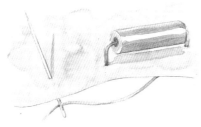

To sew bugle beads, fasten the thread as before and thread on the first bugle. With the bead lying flat on the fabric, take the needle back through to the wrong side close to the edge of the bead, and bring it up again a bugle bead's width away. Apply the next bead by taking the thread from right to left through the bead as if you were making a back stitch, and continue in the same way.

COUCHING BEADS

An alternative method of attaching beads is to thread them to make a string, which is then couched to the fabric.

Cut two lengths of invisible or matching thread. Make a knot in the end of one thread, bring it through to the surface of the fabric and thread on the beads. With another needle and the second thread, make a neat overcast stitch as closely as possible to the first bead on the string. Slide the next bead up to it and make the next stitch, and so on, following your design. To complete, finish off the couching thread neatly on the wrong side of the fabric, followed by the strung thread.

BEAD FRINGES

Decorative fringes can be created using various methods, of which the most common is to apply individually beaded strands. These can be worked in two ways.

Decide on the length required for the strands, and cut each thread to twice this length, plus a little extra to allow for sewing the finished strands in place. Thread on the beads, taking one end of the thread through the bottom bead and then both ends of the thread back up through the rest of the beads. Oversew each strand to the fabric or braid as required.

Alternatively, fasten a long thread to the fabric (see "Embroidering Beads Individually"). Thread on enough beads to make a drop of the right length. Take

the thread around the bottom bead and then back up to the top through all the other beads. Bring the thread through to the wrong side and back down again a small stitch further along the fabric. Repeat to make the next strand.

A looped fringe also makes an attractive decoration. Fasten a long thread to the fabric (see "Embroidering Beads Individually"), and thread on enough beads to creat a loop of the desired drop. Take the thread through to the wrong side in the same place, and back down again a small stitch further along.

BEAD TASSELS

Beaded tassels can look extremely effective on jewellery, soft furnishings and even clothes, and are simple to make.

Decide on the number and length of strands you require, and cut this number of threads to twice this length plus enough to allow for taking through a large bead at the top, knotting and securing to fabric. For each strand, thread on the beads, take one end of the thread through the bottom bead, then both ends back up through the rest of the beads. Complete all the strands in this way, and then take all the thread ends through a single large bead and make a secure knot. Oversew the tassel to fabric or attach it to jewellery as required.

USING FINDINGS

These metal components have a wide range of uses in jewellery making.

Head and eye pins are pre-formed lengths of soft wire, and are useful for making basic earrings. Thread on beads to the desired length, trim away any excess pin with wire-cutters, and then use pliers to turn a loop at the top end. This loop can then be joined to an ear wire.

Two or more beaded head or eye pins can be linked to make earrings, as well as bracelets and necklaces.

Large beads can be turned into pendant earrings and necklaces using a triangle bail, which is simply opened out with pliers, inserted into the bead holes and then squeezed into shape to secure.

Calottes are particularly useful when making bracelets or necklaces. They are used to conceal knots and join the thread to a jump ring, or directly to a clasp.

Bell caps can also be used to conceal knots at each end of a bracelet or necklace. Knot the threads on to an eye pin and push this through the central hole of the bell cap. Trim the pin to fit, and turn a loop in the end with pliers. You can then link this to a jump ring or directly to a clasp.

BEAD WEAVING

Beads can be woven to create the most decorative pieces in wonderful colour combinations. Experiment with different designs, and work out your pattern beforehand using coloured crayons on plain paper.

A basic bead-lace braid is an ideal first project. The thread follows a regular pattern of loops worked in a zigzag pattern to form the honeycomb effect. Begin working as many loops as necessary to create the desired width, taking the thread back through a bead (shaded in the illustration) in the previous row each time.

Follow the same method to work a wider piece, again taking the thread back through a bead in each previous row.

When the piece reaches the required size, strengthen the weaving by running an additional thread through the beads at the outer edge.

To make the fastening, knot a new thread to one end of the weaving and work a simple loop, as shown, knotting the thread end and working it back in to conceal it. Knot a new thread to the opposite end and thread on some small beads, as shown. Next, take the thread through a medium-sized bead, through a large bead, and then back through the medium-sized bead. Thread on a few more small beads to complete the loop, and finish off the thread with a knot.

MAKING YOUR OWN BEADS

Making your own beads is easy and fun. Papier mâché can be used to create light-weight beads of any size for decoration with your own designs. Marbled beads are also simple to make from Fimo or similar modelling material, as are millefiori beads, based on Venetian glass-making techniques. Pressed-cotton balls also make good bases for colourful decoration.

2 When completely dry, slice the ball in half using a craft knife and remove the Plasticine. Glue the paper shell back together, smoothing over any rough edges with another layer or two of papier mâché.

When this is dry, brush over the bead with white paint to cover the newsprint, before painting the ball with your design.

PAPIER-MACHÉ BEADS

3 When the paint is dry, pierce the bead with a needle to make holes for stringing.

1 Roll a piece of Plasticine into a ball. Cut some newspaper into small strips, paint the strips with PVA adhesive or wallpaper paste, and allow this to soak in well before covering the ball with several layers.

MARBLED BEADS

1 Knead two or three colours of Fimo modelling clay until soft and roll them into sausage shapes. Twist the sausages together. Continue to knead and twist the colours together until you achieve the marbled effect. Do not over-knead the clay, or you will lose the effect.

2 Roll out the marbled clay evenly and cut it into slices using a sharp craft knife. Roll into balls.

3 Push the beads on to cocktail sticks or wooden skewers and bake them in the oven, following the maker's instructions.

4 Paint or spray a light, even coat of varnish over the beads. Leave them to dry thoroughly. String the beads to make the jewellery or decoration of your choice.

MILLEFIORI BEADS

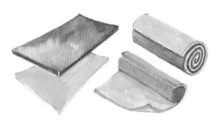

1 To make the design shown here, take Fimo modelling clay in dark blue, green,

mid-blue, red and yellow (or the colours of your choice), and knead them until soft. Roll out thin pieces of dark blue and green clay, place them together and then roll them up to make a spiral design. Roll out a sausage shape of red, and roll a thin layer of mid-blue evenly around it. Cut the sausage shape into several lengths.

2 Make similar lengths of yellow clay, and, alternating this with the blue-and-red roll, stick them around the spiral as shown. Re-roll the clay gently to maintain the shape.

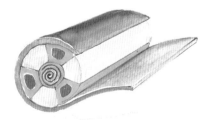

3 Roll out a thin piece of dark blue clay, and roll this around the inner colours, keeping it as even as possible. Roll out the finished sausage more thinly.

4 Cut the sausage into slices with a sharp craft knife. Use the slices to make the designs of your choice, by sticking them around a clay base as shown. Form the central holes with a pointed stick, and bake in the oven. Thread the beads on to findings to make colourful earrings, bracelets and necklaces.

PRESSED-COTTON BALLS

Pressed-cotton balls are ideal for bead making. Simply pierce your chosen balls with a needle, and then decorate them in any manner you choose. Use bright or metallic paint colours on their own, or as a base on which to add sequins or rocailles. Paint or spray the finished balls with varnish to complete.

BUTTONS

There is an amazing variety of buttons to be found in every shape, size and colour imaginable, made from many different materials including wood, horn, glass, plastic, metal and shell. They can be plain, moulded into fun shapes or carved with intricate designs, and you can even make your own.

Many people have collections of beautiful buttons, but all too often they sit unseen and unappreciated at the bottom of a box. The projects in this book will inspire you to use those buttons not merely as fastenings on clothes, but in the most innovative of ways. Antique and contemporary buttons make wonderful jewellery, for instance, and add decoration to all kinds of fashion and home accessories. The only limit to what you can do is your imagination!

SHELL BUTTONS

Shell buttons (above) have a beautiful glossy sheen. Markings can be strong and pronounced or very subtle, and the "wrong" side often looks as attractive as the right side.

NOVELTY BUTTONS

Novelty buttons (below) make ideal decoration on both children's and adults' accessories. Animals and alphabet letters used to spell out words are great fun for children's clothes.

BUTTON TYPES

There are two basic types of buttons. A shank button has a loop on the wrong side, which can be moulded from the same material, as here, or made of metal. Sew-through buttons can have any number of holes, but two or four are most commonly found today.

PLASTIC BUTTONS

Plastic buttons (left and right) can be dyed to any colour, and moulded or faceted to resemble metal, glass, ivory or almost any other material. They are much lighter and less expensive than the real thing.

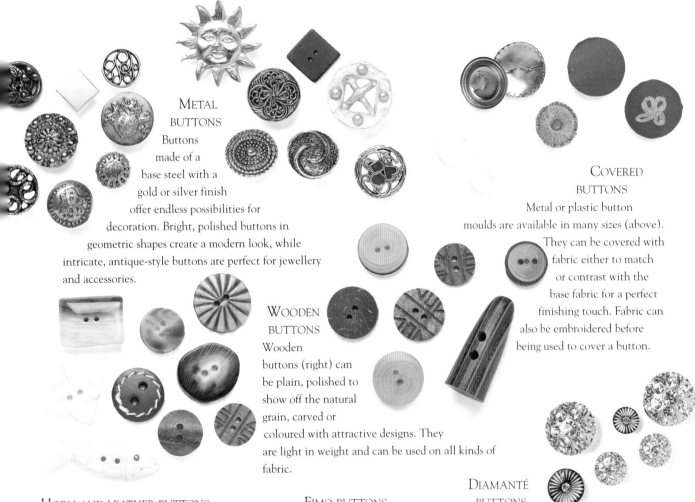

METAL BUTTONS

Buttons made of a base steel with a gold or silver finish offer endless possibilities for decoration. Bright, polished buttons in geometric shapes create a modern look, while intricate, antique-style buttons are perfect for jewellery and accessories.

COVERED BUTTONS

Metal or plastic button moulds are available in many sizes (above). They can be covered with fabric either to match or contrast with the base fabric for a perfect finishing touch. Fabric can also be embroidered before being used to cover a button.

WOODEN BUTTONS

Wooden buttons (right) can be plain, polished to show off the natural grain, carved or coloured with attractive designs. They are light in weight and can be used on all kinds of fabric.

HORN AND LEATHER BUTTONS

Horn buttons look wonderful when highly polished to show off their markings or carved with intricate designs. Leather buttons with contrasting stitching give a lovely natural feel to chunky knitwear.

FIMO BUTTONS

Marbled and millefiori buttons are simple to make from Fimo or similar modelling materials, and offer endless design and colour possibilities.

DIAMANTÉ BUTTONS

These glamorous buttons (above) are perfect for creating a glitzy evening look on clothes and accessories. They look particularly dramatic on a black or dark background, as they sparkle and catch the light.

MAKING YOUR OWN BUTTONS

Making your own buttons is easy and fun, and will give you the extra satisfaction of knowing that you have made a whole project yourself from start to finish. Fimo modelling clay is inexpensive and is available in a wide range of colours, making your options for button design almost limitless.

The finished buttons are baked in the oven to create a hardwearing finish that is suitable for a range of purposes, including jewellery, clothing and hair accessories. Bear in mind, however, that these buttons are hand washable and would therefore be unsuitable for an item that is likely to need frequent washing (unless you remove the buttons first).

embroider the fabric, do so at this stage so that you know where to position the stitching.

2 Run a gathering thread around the fabric edge and place the button at the centre. Draw up the thread so that the fabric is stretched tight across the button.

3 Snap the back of the mould on to the wrong side to fix the fabric securely.

MARBLED BUTTONS

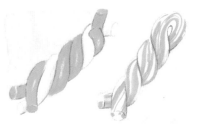

I Knead two or three colours of Fimo modelling clay until soft and roll them into equal sausage shapes. Twist the sausages together (left). Continue to knead and twist the clay colours together until you achieve the marbled effect (right). Take care not to over-knead the clay, or the colours will blend together and you will lose the effect.

COVERED BUTTONS

I Using a pair of compasses, draw a circle of a larger circumference than the button mould, and cut it out. If you wish to

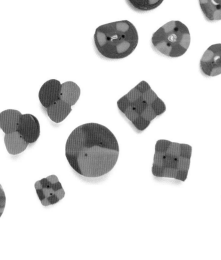

MILLEFIORI BUTTONS

1 To make the design shown here, take Fimo modelling clay in dark blue, green, mid-blue, red and yellow (or the colours of your choice), and then knead them until soft. Roll out thin pieces of dark blue and green clay, place them together and then roll them up to make a spiral design.

stick them around the spiral as shown. Re-roll the clay gently to maintain the shape.

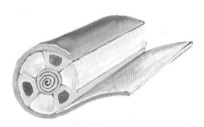

3 Roll out a thin piece of dark blue clay, and roll this around the inner colours, keeping it as even as possible. Roll out the finished sausage more thinly.

2 Roll out the marbled clay evenly and cut it into slices using a sharp craft knife.

2 Roll out a sausage shape of red, and roll a thin layer of mid-blue evenly around it. Cut the sausage shape into several lengths. Make similar lengths of yellow clay, and, alternating this with the blue-and-red roll,

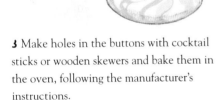

3 Make holes in the buttons with cocktail sticks or wooden skewers and bake them in the oven, following the manufacturer's instructions.

If you wish, paint or spray a light, even coat of varnish over the buttons and leave them to dry thoroughly.

4 Cut the sausage into slices with a sharp craft knife and mould them into the button shapes of your choice. Form the holes with a cocktail stick or wooden skewer, and bake the buttons in the oven

If you wish, paint or spray the buttons with a light, even coat of varnish to complete.

BOWS

Ribbons have been used through the ages to decorate clothes and furnishings. They are one of the quickest ways of enlivening a garment or household item and, nowadays, with the huge range of ribbons available, it has become even easier to pick just the right ones for your needs.

With the advent of sophisticated machines and computers, ribbon making and printing has been turned into a fine art and ribbons come in an impressive range of widths, materials and designs. Before you begin, have a good look at all the different types of ribbons on the market, pick those most suited to your project and then decide on the pattern and design.

Ribbons can be sewn or glued in position, woven to make a fabric, used as an embroidery thread or simply as a substitute for string. It is important to match your method of attaching the ribbon to the item that you are decorating. Fabric ribbons can be hand or machine-sewn in place, with their ends snipped diagonally or into inverted "V" shapes to prevent fraying. Craft or paper ribbon, on the other hand, will not fray, and can be cut, stuck and curled into shape.

As you will see from the ribbon samples shown here, the wonderful array of colours and designs means that it is never hard to find a ribbon that matches your project perfectly.

SINGLE-FACE SATIN RIBBONS

Single-face satin ribbons come in a good range of widths. They have one shiny and one dull side, and come in a wide range of plain colours and printed patterns. Single-face ribbons also sometimes have picot or metallic edges.

DOUBLE-FACE SATIN RIBBONS

Double-face satin ribbons are shiny on both sides, and are slightly thicker than the single-face variety. They are available in a good selection of plain colours, sometimes with picot or decorative edges.

POLYESTER RIBBONS

Polyester ribbons are found in an impressive range of plain colours, printed patterns and finishes, (such as crêpe), and can be combined with metallic strips or woven as tartans.

GROSGRAIN RIBBONS

Grosgrain ribbons are strong and firm with a distinctive cross-wise rib. They come in a variety of plain colours, as well as some printed or embroidered stripes and patterns. They can also have satin stripes.

TAFFETA RIBBONS

Flat and matt with a woven design, taffeta ribbons are available in many colours. They may also have a water-marked finish such as moiré, or a picot or metallic edge. Nylon taffeta is available in some wonderful gingham checks.

VELVET RIBBONS

Velvet ribbons have a raised pile and can be made in nylon or cotton. They are available as single- or double-face ribbons.

JACQUARD RIBBONS

Jacquard ribbons, woven in a similar style to the fabric of the same name, have a slightly raised design. This is often floral, but can also be geometric or metallic. Jacquard ribbons also sometimes have a picot edge.

METALLIC RIBBONS

Metallic ribbons are woven from lurex and similar metallic fibres, and come in a variety of finishes from sheer to grosgrain.

SHEER RIBBONS

Perfect for making ribbon roses, sheer, light, organdie ribbons can be printed or left plain. Some sheer ribbons have decorative or satin edges, or satin stripes running down the centre.

ROSES & ROSETTES

Ribbon roses look marvellous, whether grouped together in a vase or used to augment table decorations and presents - the possibilities are endless. The finished result will depend to a great extent on the type of ribbon that you use. Try sheer ribbon for tight, well-formed roseheads, or double-face satin ribbon for a looser interpretation. Roses can also be created from wire-edged ribbon.

Ribbon rosettes can be made from almost any type of ribbon, as they are simply gathered along one ribbon edge and pulled up into shape. To create a pompon, stick two rosettes back to back around a length of ribbon.

RIBBON ROSE ON A STEM

For each rose you will need 75 cm (30 in) of 40 mm (1½ in) wide sheer ribbon, 50 cm (20 in) of craft wire and one stem wire with green tape to cover the stem.

1 Bend over the top of the stem wire to form a loop, and hold the craft wire at the base of the loop. Lay the end of the ribbon over the loop and wrap round with craft wire to secure it.

2 Bring the ribbon up and wrap it around the stem two or three times to create the centre of the rose.

3 Begin folding the ribbon away from the centre and diagonally forward, catching it at the base each time with the craft wire. At first, fold the ribbon only slightly and wrap tightly, but then, as you work, fold more deeply and ease in more ribbon with each fold to open out the flower.

4 When the rose is the required size, bring the end of the ribbon down to the base of the flower, and bind round this to secure. Position the end of the stem binding tape directly under the rosehead. Bind the stem, attaching the tape at the base.

WIRE-EDGED RIBBON ROSE

For a large rose, cut a 100 cm (40 in) length of wired ribbon.

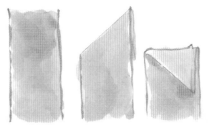

1 Fold the cut edge of the ribbon away from you at an angle of 45°. Now fold the ribbon horizontally towards you, keeping the edges even.

2 Continue to fold, making sure that you always fold away from you at a 45° angle

and that when you fold towards you, you pull the front flap forwards to make a square as shown above.

3 As you fold, try to pull the outside edge of the ribbon slightly tighter than the inner edge.

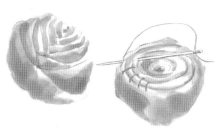

4 When you reach the end of your ribbon, use your fingers to open out the centre of the rose into a rounded flower. Hand sew the ribbon end at the base, and continue stitching as necessary to hold the rose shape.

In order to fill out the gap left underneath, push a small piece of cotton wool up into the back of the rose to hold the shape. Oversew the edges to keep the cotton wool in place.

RIBBON ROSETTE

Take a piece of ribbon approximately 50 cm (20 in) in length. Beginning with a knot, run a line of gathering stitches along one straight edge of the ribbon. Pull up the thread to form the rosette, and fasten it off securely.

POMPONS

To make a pompon, gather up two rosettes and glue them together, back to back.

RIBBON WEAVING

Ribbon weaving is similar to traditional weaving, but uses ribbon lengths instead of yarn. It provides a firm, beautifully textured fabric from which all sorts of different items can be cut and stitched. The easiest way to weave ribbons is over a background of fusible interfacing. Once the ribbons are all in place, simply fuse

them to the interfacing with a warm iron.

When weaving with ribbons, the vertical ribbons are the warp threads, while the weft refers to the ribbons that are woven from side to side across the vertical ribbons. The finished pattern can be made simple or complex by using different weaving sequences; and also by mixing

and matching different ribbon styles and widths in the same piece of work.

Ribbon weaving is simple to learn. You don't need any complicated equipment, and the finished "fabric" can be used to make cushion covers, bags, cloths and many other items.

PLAIN WEAVE

Work with satin-edged 22 mm (⅞ in) wide grosgrain ribbon in two colours.

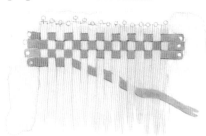

Lay the vertical ribbons out flat, side by side, alternating the colours. Working with the same ribbons horizontally, weave the first row under one, over one, under one, over one, and so on, to the end of the row. In the second row, weave the ribbon over one, under one, over one, under one, and so on, to the end of the row. The result will be smooth, plain-woven ribbon fabric.

PLAIN WEAVE USING THREE COLOURS

By mixing together two different ribbon widths – 16 mm (⅝ in) and 6 mm (¼ in) – and three different colours, you will achieve a totally different effect.

Use the same plain-weave method described left, weaving the horizontal ribbons alternately over and under the vertically placed ribbons.

TUMBLING-BLOCKS WEAVE

Team up two different pinks, both 20 mm (¾ in) wide, with a 16 mm (⅝ in) wide cream ribbon to re-create this typical patchwork design.

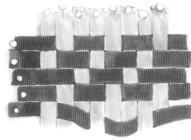

1 Lay out the vertical ribbons, and weave the horizontal ribbons through them. In the first row, work over one, under one, over two, under one, over two, and so on, to the end of the row. In the second row, work under one, over two, under one, over two, and so on, to the end, and in the third row work over two, under one, over two, under one and so on.

DIAGONAL WEAVE

Use a mix of three different-coloured ribbons for this diagonal weave – combine a plain 22 mm (⅞ in) wide satin ribbon with two 22 mm (⅞ in) wide satin-edged grosgrain ribbons.

Lay out the vertical ribbons as before. Weave the first horizontal ribbon under two, over two, under two, over two, and so on, to the end of the row. In the second row, work under one, over two, under two, over two, and so on, to the end of the row. Weave the third row over two, under two, over two, and so on, to the end. In the fourth row, work over one, under two, and so on, to the end of the row. Repeat these rows for the whole area to form the diagonal effect.

2 Finally, thread the 16 mm (⅝ in) cream ribbon diagonally to create the pattern.

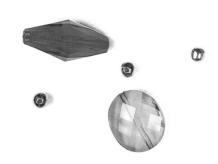

BEADS

PRACTICAL PROJECTS

BOLD BANDS

Bead-woven jewellery has been created by various cultures for centuries. Different beads and patterns have produced a great range of styles, from the work of the Native Americans to the elegant examples created by the Victorians, but the dramatically different styles use the same basic techniques.

These examples are all worked in the hand. The rings are threaded on to fine wire, and can be simple band designs or tied into decorative knots. The necklet beads are woven to cover a cord (a plastic bangle can also be used for a bracelet). Using nylon thread in a beading needle, thread on beads to form a circle which fits the base circumference exactly. Take the thread through the beads again so that the foundation thread goes around the base twice, then fasten it to the beginning of the thread. For each succeeding row, add beads one at a time, taking the thread from each new bead back through the next bead on the previous row.

If you need to join a new thread, take the end of the old thread back through the work, bringing it out between two beads. Start the new thread here, bringing it out where the beading is to continue. Tie the two ends together and trim them. When the thread is pulled tight, the knot should disappear between two beads. To finish off, take the thread back through several beads and under a firm crossing thread, then secure it with a knot.

There are many methods of bead weaving, and the floral bracelet illustrates how colours can be worked in clusters. The technique for this type of weaving is shown on page 15.

Bead weaving is a quick way of creating intricately patterned jewellery in stunning colour combinations. Bright primary colours work well, as this necklet, bracelet and two simple rings demonstrate.

Over-the-top decoration with brightly coloured "jewels" works beautifully on this simple camisole.

TOP CLASS

Bold and bedazzling, there is nothing understated about this eye-catching top. The rich jewel colours embroidered on to sophisticated cream satin create a sizzling effect that is just right for the party season.

Lay out the camisole on a flat surface and place the beads on top, working out your design before stitching them in position. You could choose a simple design of small stones to emphasize the cut cleverly, or be more outrageous and cover the piece entirely. Create a bright and jazzy top by using lots of colours together, as shown here, or achieve a softer effect with one or two colours in less vibrant shades.

The flat-backed stones have a hole on either side, just above the base, and are easy to sew on. Using a fine invisible thread and a beading needle, bring the thread up from the wrong side, take it through the holes in the stone and back through to the wrong side, pulling the thread firmly to keep the stone in place. Take care not to catch or pucker the fabric, as this will spoil the appearance of the garment. Bring the thread back up, close to the next stone, and continue working in the same way. Depending on the type of fabric and the ornateness of your design, you may find it easier to apply a lightweight iron-on interfacing to the wrong side of the fabric to give a firmer backing and to prevent the weight of the beads from dragging it down.

A unique beaded cap, finished with a trim of tiny beads on the lower edge and a copper spiral on the top.

A basic waistcoat makes an excellent foil for any form of decoration, from fabric painting to exquisite embroidery. Here, beautiful fabrics and an eclectic mix of tiny beads, sequins, found objects and embroidery materials have been combined to produce a unique piece of clothing.

VESTED INTERESTS

The secret of the beauty of this cap and waistcoat is the intricate detail on the fabric, which is simple to re-create by anyone with basic needle skills, a little imagination and plenty of patience.

Use a rich, heavy brocade for the front fabric, and top this with a layer of fine net. Cover this densely with tiny sequins and glass rocailles, and metalwork embroidery threads. Add interest by using small fluted and filigree bell caps secured with tiny beads and miniature ribbon rosettes to highlight larger beads.

This spectacular waistcoat is covered lavishly with tiny sequins, glass rocailles, bell caps, ribbon rosettes, swirls of copper and metalwork embroidery threads.

Work the main embroidery before making up and lining the waistcoat. Oversew the edges to prevent fraying while you work, and remember not to work too close to buttonholes, or to seams if you plan to machine stitch the pieces together or to add a rich corded edge. You can add detail to these areas after making up the waistcoat, taking care to stitch through the top layer of fabric only.

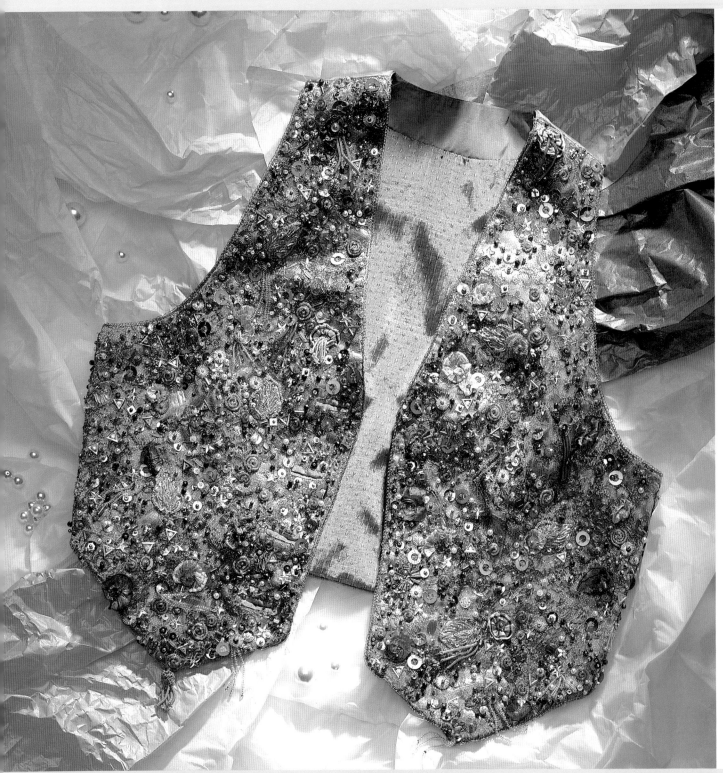

BEDAZZLING BAG

The quilted design on the bag shown here provided the inspiration for the geometric pattern. Brilliantly coloured "lozenge"-shaped beads emphasize the quilting, and glisten beautifully when they catch the light.

The slightly flattened shape of these beads lends itself to this type of decoration, as they will not catch on other objects. Large, rounder beads would create more of a problem, although small beads would look effective and could be used in greater quantities, perhaps following all the stitching lines to highlight the complete pattern.

Fabric bags are ideal for decorating in this way, as it is easy to stitch the beads in place. A leather bag is more difficult to work, but if you use a fine leather needle with its specially shaped point you can be just as creative, using beads as a trim on a bag or in an overall pattern. Intricate designs can be worked out on a paper template of the bag before starting to sew.

Use a strong cotton thread, and fasten it securely on the inside of the bag where it will not be seen. Bring the needle through to the right side at the point at which the bead is to be attached, and take it through the bead and back through to the inside. Repeat this several times to secure the bead, as you would a button, and fasten off the thread on the inside.

The brightly coloured beads used to decorate this shoulder bag set off the vivid green satin beautifully.

HEAD TURNERS

Beads are incredibly versatile, and can be used in any number of ways on hair combs, slides and ornaments.

Beads look wonderfully effective when used to trim almost any kind of hair accessory, whether to co-ordinate the accessory with a special outfit, or simply to transform daywear to evening wear.

With just a little imagination and an assortment of beads you can produce the most original hair accessories. Choose beads to go with the base material and, depending on whether this is "soft" or "hard", sew or glue the beads in place. Small beads are quite difficult to glue successfully, but look good sewn on to ornate braid or ribbon. Wrap the ribbon around the accessories and glue in place before sewing on the beads.

Try decorating tortoiseshell Alice bands, slides and hair combs with creamy pearl

beads or small rocailles. Padded-fabric Alice bands and slides look glamorous with rich, antiqued gold or silver beads, and diamanté roundels add a touch of sparkle for evening wear. Fabric scrunchies can be edged with small beads, and plastic canvas cut into barrette shapes and decorated with ornate bead work.

Experiment and plan your designs before securing the beads in place. This is not always easy on narrow, curved surfaces, so use double-sided adhesive tape to hold the beads temporarily. If you are sewing the beads, you may find a fine, curved needle useful for awkward angles. Choose a matching or invisible thread, or add some extra texture to the design by sewing on the beads with fine ribbon or raffia.

Alice bands and scrunchies make ideal candidates for bead decoration. (Left)

A black-velvet headband teamed with gold beading makes an elegant evening

accessory; (centre) sparkling purple and green beads interspersed with

strings of small beads enliven a plain headband; and (below) a simple edging

of gold beads transforms a scrunchy in brown velvet.

These Victorian-style food covers with their pretty bead trims are ideal for draping over basins and jugs to keep insects at bay when dining outside on a summer's day.

CHARMING COVERS

The Victorians delighted in pretty yet practical accessories for the home, and, in the days before refrigerators, these lovely crocheted covers were an attractive and efficient way of keeping flies away from food and drink. Beads were used to decorate almost anything, and here they add a charming finishing touch while also keeping the covers in place. Dining *al fresco* is frequently spoiled by flies and other insects making a nuisance of themselves, so whether you are hosting an elegant tea party or a fun barbecue, these appealing covers are the perfect solution.

These nostalgic examples have been hand-crocheted in a fine cotton yarn to create a pretty, lacy effect. Once the main fabric has been worked, the yarn is finished off and the beads threaded on to a new piece of yarn before the edging is added, so it is easy to add beads to a bought or already completed piece of crochet.

White fabric is traditionally used, but you could of course work the covers in any colour to co-ordinate with your favourite china. You could also add beaded fringes to scraps of lace fabric or pretty fabric tablemats and coasters to complete the look and to stop them from blowing away in the breeze.

Crocheted covers edged with hanging beads make a practical and pretty feature at an outdoor meal.

Impress your friends and spice up your dining-table with high-style salt and

pepper pots. This unusual use of beads will turn the most ordinary condiment

set into a real conversation piece!

SENSATIONAL SEASONINGS

The finished look of your salt and pepper pots can be as conservative or as wild as you choose, and worked in colours to co-ordinate with anything from your table settings to your interior décor. More elaborate effects can be achieved by covering the pots completely.

Tip some beads on to a saucer and mix the colours thoroughly. Apply a strong, waterproof, clear-drying adhesive to the pot, working on one section at a time and taking care to cover only the area to be decorated. Lay out some newspaper and, when the glue is tacky, hold the pot over the paper and sprinkle over the beads.

Leave the pot until the glue is completely dry before starting to work on another section. When the glue is dry, brush over the beads gently with your fingers to dislodge any that are loose. Add a finishing touch by gluing seed pearls randomly over the beaded sections. Wash the pots carefully by hand in tepid (but not hot) water, and allow them to dry.

Decorated with a mixture of tiny silver and

crystal rocailles and highlighted with pearls,

these basic salt and pepper pots would look

stunning in any setting.

LIGHT SHOW

A heavy fringe of crystal beads creates a look reminiscent of a bygone era on this simple glass shade.

Lampshades are one of the easiest home accessories to customize with beads, enabling you to put your own creative stamp on an interior.

The rich-looking bead fringe on the left was worked in a simple pattern using colours to co-ordinate with the shade. Two differently patterned strings were alternated all round, each being threaded on to cotton, which hangs more freely than nylon, and worked from the bottom upwards.

Cut a piece of braid or tape to fit the shade, allowing for securing and turning in

raw edges. For each string, cut a length of cotton a little more than twice the required depth. Thread one end through the base bead, then both ends through the rest of the beads. Overstitch the thread to the wrong side of the braid so that the top bead sits just below the braid. To finish, wrap the braid around the bottom of the shade and stitch it securely in place. Alternatively, use double-sided adhesive tape to secure the braid on the shade.

To make the trim for the parchment shade opposite, string the beads on to

nylon thread – the finished
length will need to be the circumference of the bottom edge of
the shade plus at least half as
much again, depending on the
width and depth of the drop. To
secure the string, first pierce holes at
regular intervals around the bottom of the
shade, through the binding, to prevent the
shade from tearing. Next, fold the nylon
thread double at the point the drop is to
start, and push this loop through
the hole to the wrong
side. Overstitch the
loop firmly to the
binding, adding
a small blob of
glue to secure.
Once the string
is in place, glue
wooden disc beads
over the holes to give
a neat finish.

A parchment shade

enhanced with a

scalloped fringe of

rich wooden beads.

TREE TREASURES

The beautiful bead

and sequin

decorations opposite

are simple to make

and would grace any

Christmas tree.

Decking the Christmas tree with your own hand-made ornaments will create an attractive and original centrepiece. Use beads and sequins to produce traditional shapes in seasonal colours.

It is easy to turn pressed-cotton or styrofoam balls into stunning baubles using beads and sequins. Create an ornate finish by pinning sequins in rows all over the ball with classic flat-head or glass-head pins, and either trim the bauble with ribbon or make your own braid by weaving tiny rocailles together. You could produce a simpler look by trimming the plain ball with a woven bead braid, or by painting the ball itself gold, silver or any other seasonal colour first.

Bugle beads make beautiful stars. Use invisible or matching thread and begin by threading on six bugles, taking the end of the thread back through the first one. Draw up the beads into a hexagon shape. Put two further bugles on to the thread, then take the thread back through one of the bugles forming the hexagon as if making a backstitch. Take the thread all the way through the next bugle on the hexagon, then thread on two more bugles and make the backstitch. Continue all round until you have a six-pointed star. Fasten the thread ends securely, and make a hanging loop with new thread from one point.

The pretty icicles shown opposite are made using special beads, which sit neatly on top of one another to form the icicle shape. To make stars, glue five same-sized beads together in a ring. When dry, make the points by gluing smaller and smaller beads together, radiating out from the central beads.

Hand-knitted in simple stocking stitch in a standard double-knitting yarn, these delightful baubles add a dash of colour to the tree at Christmas, and are also perfect for using up oddments of wool.

FESTIVE BAUBLES

An inspired choice of yarn can produce stunning effects on these highly original Christmas decorations. A luxurious chenille in brilliant jewel colours creates a rich velvety bauble, for example. Silky ribbon yarns or glittering metallics have a lustrous sheen which adds a touch of glamour, while white mohair resembles soft fluffy snowballs, especially if brushed.

To knit the decorations, use the recommended needle size and tension quoted on the ball band (although for these fun baubles, traditional techniques can be ignored as long as you are happy with the resulting knitted fabric). For a simple stocking-stitch bauble, cast on between 11 and 15 stitches, depending on the yarn and size of ball required. Increase in every stitch on the first (knit) row to double the initial number of stitches. Knit a further 14 to 18 rows (or as desired) in stocking stitch (knit one row, purl one row), ending on a purl row.

On the next row, decrease back to the original number of stitches by knitting two together across the row. Break the yarn, leaving a long "tail", and thread this back through the remaining stitches. Slip the stitches off the needle.

Using a tapestry needle threaded with the same yarn, run a row of gathering stitches along the cast-on edge, draw it up tightly and fasten it off. Stitch the side seam, matching the row ends, and turn the fabric through to the right side. Stuff the bauble with wadding. Pull up the length of yarn at the top, gathering the stitches tightly, and fasten it off. Make a hanging loop in matching yarn or metallic thread and secure this to the top.

Decorate each bauble extravagantly with beads and sequins. You can either sew these on, or glue them in place using an appropriate craft adhesive.

Bright knitted ornaments trimmed with beads make a lovely change from shop-bought tree decorations, and sparkle beautifully under the lights.

The gentle sound of tinkling windchimes has

a wonderfully soothing effect,

reminding one of mystical, far-off

lands. Hang them in

windows or doorways to catch the slightest

breath of air.

Simple bone beads,

some carved with

exotic patterns,

along with cinnabar

and silver beads,

CHIMERICAL CHIMES

The mix of subtle, neutral colours high-lighted with cinnabar and silver empha-sizes the design of these simple chimes. They were hung from a cheap plastic cur-tain ring bound with fine string to enhance the natural theme. You could steep the string in cold tea for a few hours to darken it subtly, or use raffia, twine or brightly coloured cord to bind the ring if you prefer.

For the outer ring, make up six bead strings on strong, invisi-ble nylon line, each measuring approx-imately 25 cm (10 in) when completed. To

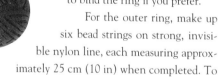

do this, cut the six threads into lengths of 60 cm (24 in), fold each in half and take one end of the thread through the bell first and then both ends through the rest of the beads. Tie and knot each of these securely to the plastic ring. Bind string tightly round the ring to cover it completely, tak-ing the string across the centre and back again to form the middle bar.

To make up the centrepiece, start with three strings. Bring these together at the top by threading all the ends together through more beads. Plait three lengths of string together to make the hanging thread, and knot this and the centrepiece to the middle bar. The finished wind-chimes will add a restful touch to any cor-ner of your home.

make beautiful

windchimes. Hang

them by a door or

window and enjoy

their soft sounds

as they sway in

the breeze.

BUTTONS

PRACTICAL PROJECTS

Spice up a plain but brightly coloured jacket by adding more colour with a novel button trim. Stunning contrasts work well together, giving the jacket a totally new look.

JAZZY JACKET

Rows of colourful buttons on the pockets, with larger buttons on the cuffs, give this plain blue jacket a really stylish finish.

Italian designers are renowned for producing clothes with both style and humour, and it was their inspired use of buttons as decoration on clothes that influenced this jacket. You can use buttons in lots of unusual ways to add designer detail and to make a more eye-catching feature of an ordinary element. Necklines can be prettily enhanced, while hems and waistbands can be emphasized by outlining them with attractive buttons in toning or clashing colours. Collars, cuffs and pockets can be given the same treatment – cover them lavishly with buttons for a really ornate finish, or just dot the buttons about for a more understated look.

Brightly coloured buttons have been used to decorate the pocket tops and cuffs on this jacket. Using bold colour on top of another bold colour usually requires some courage, but the result can be sensational, as you can see here. The buttons look good enough to eat, like brightly coloured sweets, and add a brilliant jazzy finish. For those who prefer a less striking design, simply swapping the original buttons for more colourful ones will add some individual flair.

The buttons can have shank or hole fittings and need to be sewn in place overlapping each other to cover the area completely. If you decorate the pocket tops of a jacket, be sure to sew the buttons securely, as they will get quite a lot of wear with hands going in and out of them frequently.

An ordinary dinner jacket comes to life with the help of some strategically placed diamanté buttons. These add wonderful light-catching sparkles, and contrast beautifully with the black fabric. Other buttons could be substituted for a different look – gold or bright colours would be very effective.

Having scoured nearly-new shops, charity shops and various fairs, I discovered this classic dinner jacket with matching trousers at a car-boot sale. The suit was a real find at a bargain price. It was in good condition and, after dry-cleaning, looked brand new. Many people throw out amazingly good clothes, and it is easy to become addicted to searching out original pieces to customize by adding your own personal mark.

This jacket was given a more feminine feel by decorating the silky satin revers with an assortment of diamanté and modern clear perspex buttons to add glamour, while still retaining the sleek, stylish, tailored look. The jacket originally fastened with a traditional

passementerie braided button which was rather the worse for wear, so this was replaced with a single spectacular diamanté button to complete the sophisticated look.

A more understated effect can be achieved by simply swapping the original fastening buttons and those on the cuffs for more elaborate or opulent ones. You could add further interest by decorating the breast pocket and perhaps the side pockets with additional buttons. The diamanté buttons used here add a touch of sparkle, but pretty mother-of-pearl buttons, with their lustrous sheen, or antique silver or gold buttons, would look just as stunning.

On this jacket, the buttons on the revers were sewn in place individually with a beading needle and a fine invisible thread of the type often used for machine embroidery. A single strand of silk embroidery thread in a matching colour could also be used. The important point is to cause as little damage as possible to the fabric, in case you decide one day to revert to the original look.

DAZZLING DJ

Glittering diamanté buttons add jazz and pizzazz to a second-hand

dinner jacket, turning it into a designer-style original that is perfect

for glamorous evenings out.

NATURAL WINNER

Waistcoats are extraordinarily versatile items of clothing – they can be sharp and tailored, casual and unstructured, or dressy and elegant, and look as good worn with a business suit as they do with jeans.

A perennial fashion favourite, the waistcoat has come a long way from its traditional roots – the simple tailored version worn under a suit jacket has been banished to the city and has made way for a more colourful cousin. A waistcoat can be dressed up or down to suit the occasion and the character of its owner, turning it into an accessory rather than just an item of clothing.

Inspired by attractive but expensive designs available in the shops, this waistcoat was made up in a loose-weave raw silk from a simple dressmaking pattern. The soft beige fabric toned

beautifully with a set of horn buttons that I had in my collection, but some wooden buttons and others which had a natural feel also complemented the material particularly well, so I decided to use all the buttons to create a totally original and eye-catching waistcoat with a fashionable natural theme.

In this instance, the waistcoat was already completed, so the buttons had to be added afterwards. The tricky part is sewing them to the top fabric only so that ugly stitching does not show through on the lining, which would prevent the garment from being worn open. You may find it easier to make up the waistcoat only partially, joining the lining just to the front edges before adding the button decoration.

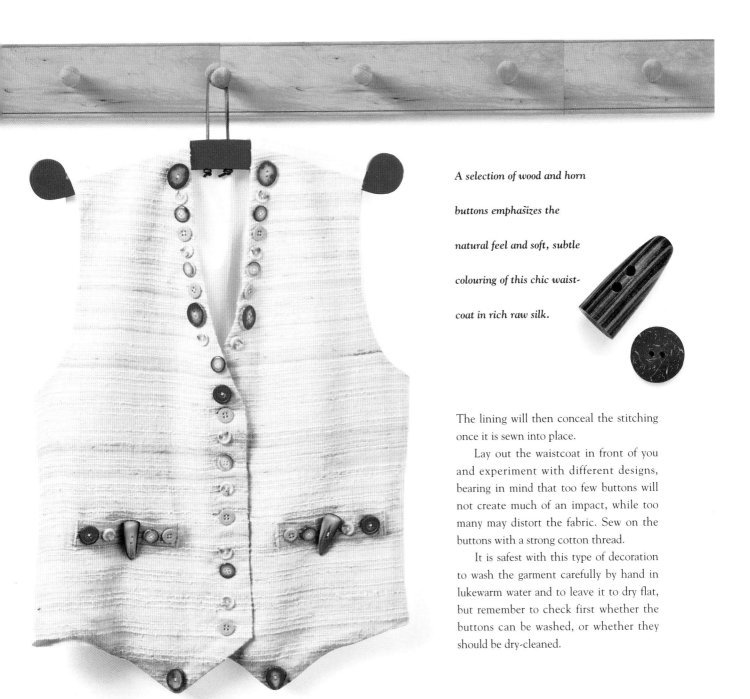

A selection of wood and horn buttons emphasizes the natural feel and soft, subtle colouring of this chic waist-coat in rich raw silk.

The lining will then conceal the stitching once it is sewn into place.

Lay out the waistcoat in front of you and experiment with different designs, bearing in mind that too few buttons will not create much of an impact, while too many may distort the fabric. Sew on the buttons with a strong cotton thread.

It is safest with this type of decoration to wash the garment carefully by hand in lukewarm water and to leave it to dry flat, but remember to check first whether the buttons can be washed, or whether they should be dry-cleaned.

A plain-coloured waistcoat can be transformed with the help of an eye-catching button design. Light, bright buttons look particularly effective on black fabric for a special occasion.

PEARLY QUEEN

This plain black waist-coat has been decorated with small mother-of-pearl buttons clustered in stylized floral motifs, each of which is high-lighted with delicate seed pearls.

Plain black fabric can be decorated in all manner of ways to create totally different looks. Mother-of-pearl buttons and seed pearls were used here, but small gold buttons and rocaille beads could also be incorporated into this or a similar design for a more ornate and dressy finish.

This simple waistcoat was made using a basic paper pattern. First cut out all the pieces from the fabric and lining material, and then lay out the two front pieces. Remembering to allow for the seams, place the buttons on the front pieces

and experiment with different patterns and designs until you have decided exactly what you want. Mark the position of all the buttons with tailor's chalk, and sew them in place before joining the front pieces to the lining (in this way, the unattractive stitching on the wrong side will be concealed inside the lining). If you wish to update a waistcoat that you already have in your wardrobe, as in the previous project, be sure to make tiny, neat stitches to prevent an ugly finish that would show if the waistcoat were worn unbuttoned.

Complete the waistcoat, following the instructions on the pattern, and then wear your finished design with pride in the knowledge that it is a one-off original.

Square and round buttons in varying sizes highlight the cable pattern on this hand-made sweater. The tassels, which were simply made from three bead strings threaded in place under the button, add the perfect finishing touch.

SILVER HIGHLIGHTS

see how they look. Let the design and pattern on the sweater guide you, and try to highlight any interesting detail. If you are decorating a plain stocking-stitch sweater, be brave and dot buttons all over it, or create an intricate patchwork effect. Choose buttons of a suitable weight for the type of garment – big, heavy, metal buttons look best on chunky wool, while mother-of-pearl or glass buttons are ideal for finer yarns.

Once you have decided on the design, sketch it out roughly on paper and then, following this guide, sew on each button individually using a strong thread in a colour to match the garment.

The finished sweater will need to be washed with care by hand and dried flat, or dry-cleaned (refer to the recommendation on the ball band if the sweater is a hand-knit, or to the manufacturer's instructions if it is a bought item). Be sure to bear the aftercare in mind when selecting your buttons, as this will affect your choice.

Give a favourite sweater a bright new look by personalizing it with decorative buttons. Choose interesting shapes and textures to add designer flair, or bright, clashing colours for a more fun look.

Buttons can be added as decoration to both bought and hand-knitted sweaters. Use the buttons as simple trims around collars, cuffs and welts, or to accentuate the texture, as in this example.

Choose colours to co-ordinate or to add richness. Wood and horn buttons go well with cream or tweedy Aran knits, for instance. The lustre of shell buttons enhances almost any garment, as do precious metals, especially those with antiqued finishes. Primary colours in bold shapes provide dramatic contrast to plain black or dark fabric such as navy or bottle green.

Lay the sweater out flat and experiment, placing buttons here and there to

Give last season's hat a brand new look by using buttons to add style and humour. Be bold and daring or subtle and understated with your design, and create an original head-turning accessory!

Buttons sewn to hat bands can create a range of effects. Natural-coloured buttons complement the "pot" hat above perfectly, and wood and horn buttons suit the trilby on the right.

HAT TRICKS

A few buttons and a little imagination can transform a very ordinary hat into a trendsetter with designer flair. You could cover the whole crown lavishly with buttons, creating a real conversation piece, or, if you feel less adventurous, you could simply highlight the brim or band.

Choose the buttons to complement the style of the hat, as well as the occasion. It is a good idea to tack the buttons in place on one thread to check the design first, before sewing each in their final position individually. Use a strong thread in a matching colour.

The striking flower buttons decorating the band on the cream straw hat below add a lovely summery feel that would be perfect for a wedding or christening, or even a day at the races. Sportier felt hats, such as the one shown below left, can be trimmed with wood and horn buttons in natural colours, with the buttons positioned on one side of the band in place of a more traditional feather or flower decoration.

The brown felt "pot" hat on the right makes an ideal candidate for fun decoration – buttons can be sewn all round the rim, or even all over the crown, as shown here. The buttons on this hat have been sewn randomly, but you could sew them in patterns for a more "structured" look.

The crown of the "pot" hat above has been covered in a delightful assortment of quirky buttons collected over a period of time. They are of all shapes and sizes, and add a humorous touch that is both stylish and chic. On the other "pot" hat, on the opposite page, wood, leather and horn buttons have been used with the occasional golden highlight to decorate the brim and set off the dark brown base colour beautifully.

You can have a lot of fun with button decoration on hats, and could even decorate interchangeable bands to give the same hat a totally different look to suit both your mood and the occasion. Just let your imagination run wild and create your own totally original accessories.

TASTEFULLY TRIMMED

The ingenious use of buttons for trimming and decoration can refresh the most jaded or out-of-date clothes and accessories, giving them a stylish new lease of life.

Revamp an old leather belt with interesting button detail. Groups of buttons have been put together to create this simple design.

The fringed trim on this sweater was created by threading buttons together to make a long necklace. The buttons chosen were of different shapes and sizes, but were all made of wood, horn and leather to create a natural effect which complements the beige colour of the sweater.

You will need to work with two threads to hold the buttons in place. Start one thread by bringing it up through a hole in the first button, then put it down through the hole in the next button, and so on. The second thread runs parallel to the first but is worked the other way – that is, down through the first hole, up through the second hole, and so on. Leaving a small gap between each button, thread on as many as you require for the length, alternating the styles and shapes along the "necklace". Knot each end. Next, cut smaller lengths of string: you will need one piece for each gap between buttons. Fold each length in half and tie it over the two threads between each button as you would a gift tag – push the looped end under the threads, and then bring the other two ends up over the two threads and pull the ends through the loop. Knot to secure. Trim the fringe and knot wooden beads to the end of each "tassel" to finish.

To decorate a belt such as the

The neckline of this plain V-neck sweater is enhanced with buttons made of wood, horn and leather. String emphasizes the "natural" effect, and also echoes the stitching on the leather buttons, setting off the rich brown colour scheme perfectly.

one shown on the left, the buttons can be glued in place, but, for a more durable finish, it is wise to stitch them in position. When decorating a thick leather belt, you may need to use a bradawl (see page 8) to start each hole. Work out the design first, and then sew each button in position using a strong thread and a special leather needle.

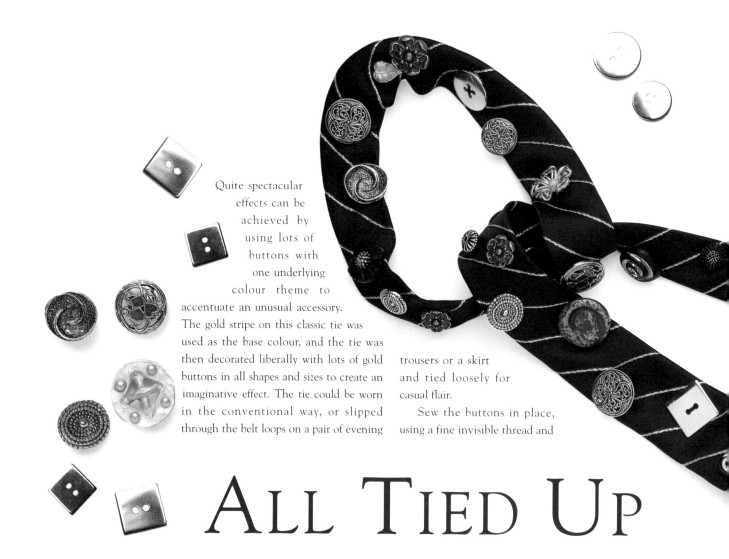

Quite spectacular effects can be achieved by using lots of buttons with one underlying colour theme to accentuate an unusual accessory. The gold stripe on this classic tie was used as the base colour, and the tie was then decorated liberally with lots of gold buttons in all shapes and sizes to create an imaginative effect. The tie could be worn in the conventional way, or slipped through the belt loops on a pair of evening trousers or a skirt and tied loosely for casual flair.

Sew the buttons in place, using a fine invisible thread and

ALL TIED UP

Take one basic tie, decorate it with a large assortment of gold buttons, and you

have a brand new look that will add dash to your wardrobe and a touch of

humour to any social occasion.

This striped tie is lavishly

decorated with varied gold

buttons. A good starting

point is to pick out a colour

from the design on the tie,

or from the

background, and to

use this as

the basis

for your button

colour theme.

taking tiny stitches.

The buttons can be sewn randomly all over the tie, as in the design shown here, or you could position them more uniformly, perhaps using just a few in one area to create a focal point. The intended purpose of the tie will obviously influence the placing of the buttons to some extent, so bear this in mind when you are planning your design. Choose rich metallic finishes and jewel-like colours for evenings, and bright primary colours or wooden buttons for day wear.

Use this idea to inspire you to create original accessories that you can be sure no one else will be wearing. Have fun playing around with different ideas and designs, and experimenting with colours and patterns, until you come up with something really effective. There are lots of other accessories which can be given the same treatment, such as scarves, stoles, hats, gloves, evening bags and even shoes, and there are more ideas for some of these throughout the book. You will soon realize that the possibilities are endless, and you will find yourself looking for different and unusual buttons everywhere you go.

Buttons can be used to trim many different hair accessories,

giving them a unique personal stamp or simply transforming them from practical

daytime to more sophisticated evening wear.

HAIR DRESSING

Tortoiseshell-effect slides and combs look particularly attractive when combined with shell or pearl buttons. Padded black velvet or satin Alice bands look glamorous with sparkling diamanté and metallic buttons for evening wear. You could even continue the theme on other accessories to go with your outfit, such as a bag or shoes – refer to other projects in the book for ideas.

To make your own head-turning accessories, you need to experiment and plan your designs before securing the buttons. This is not

always very easy on narrow, curved surfaces, but double-sided adhesive tape is perfect for holding the buttons in position temporarily while you work out the design.

When you come to sewing, you may find a curved needle useful to deal with any awkward angles. You can use thread to add some texture to the design by sewing on the buttons

with fine ribbon or raffia, for example, or you can simply choose a matching colour or use an invisible thread.

For gluing, it is essential to use a glue that is suitable for the materials with which you are working, and to ensure that both surfaces are free from dust and grease. Wiping the surfaces with a lint-free cloth dipped in white spirit is one way of doing this. You may need to roughen the surfaces of some plastic materials slightly with emery paper before gluing – this will give a key and will ensure good contact.

Buttons make

wonderful additions to

all kinds of hair

accessories, from combs

to Alice bands. Choose

toning or contrasting

button colours to suit

your outfit and

your mood.

Bold gold and black buttons on a velvet band make a stunning bracelet. This could be complemented by matching earrings or even a choker necklace.

BROOCH & BRACELET

Button jewellery is really easy to make and produces truly original and individual pieces. No two designs will be the same, especially if you use antique buttons.

It is possible to make attractive jewellery from just a small assortment of buttons by using a little imagination and ingenuity. The bracelet shown opposite was made with a mixture of antique and modern buttons to create a beautiful finished piece. To start the design, choose one or two buttons that you really like and create a colour scheme around them. Once you begin to see the possibilities, you will soon become addicted to searching out button shops and stalls in every town that you visit! Antique fairs, car-boot sales and jumble sales are other great sources for old buttons. Search through the clothes for interesting and unusual designs which could be snipped off and used for decorative purposes.

The buttons for this bracelet were sewn on to an elasticated velvet band to create a chunky, evening effect with a designer feel. The buttons were overlapped so that they totally covered the band for a really rich, ornate look.

The button brooch on this page was inspired by a wonderful seashell button

which, alongside the mother-of-pearl and starfish buttons, created a seashore theme. Filmy ribbon conceals the cardboard base and gives a seaweed effect to tie in with the rest of the design. A scattering of small gold beads creates the impression of sand.

Let the buttons do the inspiring. Few people who become interested in buttons can resist building up a large collection, and you will find that, once you have spotted one or two buttons on a particular theme, you will start discovering them everywhere. Then you will find exactly the right button that could be worked into a design to set it off perfectly and create a really dazzling piece of jewellery.

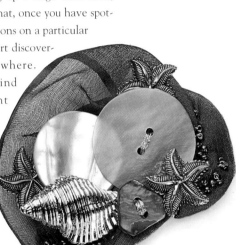

This delicate seashore brooch looks very intricate but is extremely easy to make. The mother-of-pearl button provides a perfect foil to the bright gold shell and starfish.

Colourful novelty buttons

enhanced with embroidered stems

make this plain white child's shirt

really attractive. Buttons can be used

in this way on almost any item of clothing.

The easiest way to give clothes a brighter look is to replace boring and uninspiring buttons with fun novelty versions. These are now available in all shapes and sizes and in fabulous jazzy colours that kids will love. Most are designed especially for children's clothing, so they should be both safe and washable, but check first if you are in any doubt.

SUNFLOWER SHIRT

Bright and shiny novelty buttons are a great way of personalizing children's clothes. Ordinary chain-store buys can be

turned into desirable designer originals with very little time and effort.

With a little imagination, you can make an item really special by using the buttons to create a design that is a work of art. You can see on the shirt shown here that these sunny flower buttons look great with stylized stems and leaves embroidered to highlight the effect. Taking the buttons on to the pocket and collar and adding two ladybird buttons continues the theme.

Use the buttons to inspire added detail. Ducks and boats can have wavy lines embroidered underneath them to look like the ripples on a pond, for example, and simple stars can be made to look like shooting stars with a few small beads or stitches. There are all kinds of

possibilities, and if you check out the novelty buttons at good haberdashers you are sure to find inspiration and come up with lots of your own unique and fun ideas.

Fruit-shaped buttons are easy to find, and can be used to create a fruit-bowl motif on a pocket, with different fruits used for the buttons and on the collar. Alphabet buttons are also widely available, and are fun when combined to spell out names, while numbers can be used to create a clock face on casual wear such as sweatshirts. Add a touch of humour to a school shirt or jacket with buttons in the shapes of pencils and pencil sharpeners.

Patchwork combines

beautifully with buttons

to give a "homely"

feel. The buttons

on this cover

were sewn

through all the layers to

create a traditional

quilted effect.

Patchwork, one of the oldest of home crafts, uses scraps of fabrics cut into shapes to form a pattern. These are then sewn together to form a whole piece of fabric with a mosaic effect, which can range from being subtle and understated to really bold and bright. Many different pattern shapes are used in traditional patchwork designs, but one of the simplest is based on the square, as used here.

This straightforward pattern is perfect for the beginner, provided that each square is cut to exactly the same measurement. You will find templates for the pattern shapes at most good craft shops, and using these

The craft of patchwork is traditionally used to create pretty bedcovers,

cushion covers and many other attractive items. This charming and simple-to-make

quilt illustrates how effective the combination of patchwork and buttons can be.

QUILTED TREASURE

makes cutting the fabric into identical, regular shapes a much simpler task.

This delightful cover was made from a pretty patchwork of co-ordinating fabrics in bright fresh colours, ingeniously trimmed with buttons to create the quilted effect. Join the squares together to make a patchwork fabric that is the required size for your project. When you have finished this, join it to the backing fabric, with polyester wadding sandwiched between the two layers. Stitch all the layers together and sew bias binding around the edges to neaten them.

To complete the cover, sew buttons at the points at which the corners of the

squares meet, sewing through the wadding and pulling the thread tight to create the quilted effect. As a decorative twist on the cover shown, stranded embroidery cotton of a contrasting colour was taken through each button and tied, leaving long, wispy ends. Make a small knot in each of the ends to prevent the cotton from fraying and working loose.

The finished cover is charming and would look good on any bed. It is, however, important to point out that it is not advisable to decorate babies' cot covers with button trims, just in case the buttons were pulled off and swallowed. The cover should be washed carefully by hand.

Interior décor can be updated and given designer detail with the canny use of unusual buttons. These terrific tiebacks add subtle glamour and style to the plainest of curtains, without looking "over the top".

TERRIFIC TIEBACKS

Buttons can be used effectively in many interesting ways, adding an individual artistic touch to a variety of items. Once you begin to let your imagination run riot, you will come up with all sorts of original ideas to enhance your home.

The texture of furnishing cord in soft, subtle colours sets off the pearly sheen on this collection of shell and mother-of-pearl buttons for attractive tiebacks which complement the fabric of the curtains. It is also a unique way of putting a collection of

beautiful buttons permanently on show for all to admire, and is sure to be a real conversation starter.

The buttons can be sewn on to cover the cord completely, or to form a focal point of interest. You could also decorate fabric tiebacks in the same way to create an equally stylish effect. Choose buttons in colours to co-ordinate with the room for a harmonious look, but go for striking contrasts of colour if you wish to create a really dramatic impact.

The buttons on this cord tieback were sewn in position using a cream stranded embroidery cotton. Working with three strands together, take the thread through the centre of the cord and bring it out at the point at which the next button is to be secured. The finished cord can be topped off with an ornate tassel.

There are many other accessories for the home which can be given an interesting new look with some simple button decoration – just let your imagination run free and don't be frightened to be inventive.

Buttons in subtle, natural shades sewn on to furnishing cord give an elegant feel to these pale blue curtains. An elaborate tassel adds the perfect finishing touch.

HOT SPOTS

Bring a dash of style and a splash of colour to a child's

room by cleverly trimming a variety of accessories with

bold buttons in bright, sizzling hues.

Imaginative use of buttons in stunning colour combinations can achieve spectacular results. Once you start, you will find that even the most ordinary of objects can be given a jazzy new look using the simplest of decoration, as shown here. Toy boxes and other accessories can be revamped with buttons glued on as decoration, but be sure to use a tough epoxy adhesive so that inquisitive little fingers can't remove them.

The buttons on this lampshade and curtain look like a spattering of brightly coloured sweets or polka dots. The pattern on the curtain was worked out roughly first, and the position of the buttons marked with tailor's chalk. They were then sewn on in the traditional way to make them as secure and as child-proof as possible. If you are using buttons with shanks, choose a thread in a colour to match the fabric, but buttons with central holes can be sewn with brightly coloured contrasting thread to add extra zest to the finished appearance.

The same design was used to great effect on the lampshade. Here the buttons were made to look as if they were sewn in place, but they were in fact glued. Take a bright contrasting thread through the holes several times and knot it securely on the wrong side, and then use a strong, heat-resistant craft adhesive to glue the buttons firmly in position.

The beauty of these ideas is that, when the children get bored with the design, or grow out of it, the accessories can easily be replaced at little cost. Unpick the thread carefully and remove the buttons from the curtain and lampshade when you feel like a change, and re-use them for some of the other projects shown in this book!

The bright primary
colours of these
buttons really sing out
against the rich
cobalt-blue
background of the
curtain, and would
make a perfect corner
for a child's bedroom.

This romantic work of art was inspired by the Victorian era, and

comprises a collection of old buttons, a couple of pieces of lace collected on my travels and a treasured card.

PRETTY AS A PICTURE

These lovely buttons lay unused and unappreciated at the bottom of a needlework box. I discovered the lace in Amsterdam in a shop selling bric-à-brac and thought that it was too precious to use on something frivolous, while the card, from a special friend, could not be discarded yet had no worthwhile use. Displayed together, they make the most enchanting picture of mementoes and treasures that would otherwise gather dust.

Having chosen your frame, you need to work out the size of your picture. Cut out a piece of craft interfacing to fit inside the frame exactly, and then a piece of fabric 5 cm (2 in) wider than this. Fold the fabric over the interfacing and stitch to secure it in place, making sure that the stitches don't show through on the right side. Arrange your treasures on the fabric, and stitch or glue them in place. Mark the position of the card with tailor's chalk, and then sew down the lace with invisible thread. The buttons for this picture were stitched on individually using embroidery silk, but, if you have a collection of antique buttons still on their original cards, they can look attractive displayed in groups and glued in place complete with the backing card. Use a clear-drying adhesive that is suitable for fabric both for the card keepsake and the buttons. Leave the picture until it is completely dry, press it carefully if necessary, and then place it in the picture frame and secure.

Treasure samplers such as this one make wonderful personalized gifts, especially as bridal or christening presents.

CREATIVE CARDS

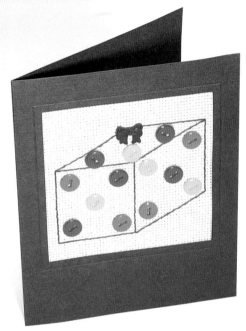

Interesting buttons can be used to make individual greetings cards with truly personal messages of good wishes, and in different styles to suit every possible occasion.

This small card made with white duck buttons positioned on a navy background is simple but very effective, and could be used for any festive occasion.

Card blanks are available in a variety of sizes and colours, and are perfect for making your own personalized greetings cards to send with love to your nearest and dearest. Decorate them with brightly coloured novelty buttons to welcome a new baby, to wish someone a happy birthday or just to say hello. You can draw extra detail on the front of the card blanks to complement the button design, and the borders look very

Bright, primary-coloured buttons resemble jazzy spotted wrapping-paper on the embroidered present, and would enhance any Christmas or birthday greeting.

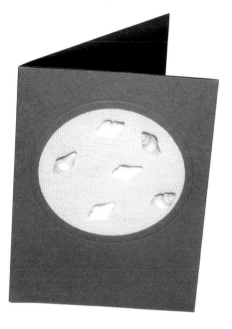

fabrics can also be used to set off the pattern of the buttons. Work out the button design before stitching the embroidery design, marking the position of each button with tailor's chalk. Use stranded silk or cotton embroidery thread for words to suit the occasion, using cross stitch or a mix of stitches if preferred. There are many books and magazines available with charts of alphabets and borders which will inspire and help you. When the embroidery is complete, sew the buttons securely in place and mount the fabric inside a card blank, gluing it to secure.

Pastel-coloured shell buttons make a pretty design on this circular card blank. You can buy card blanks in many different shapes and sizes to suit all your design ideas.

effective when highlighted with gold or silver marker pens.

There is such a wonderful range of novelty buttons on the market that you will never be short of inspiration for creating cards suitable for any occasion. Flower buttons are available in a range of shapes and sizes, and these could be worked into small bouquets or placed as an arrangement in a vase. The only limit to what you can do is your imagination!

If you sew the buttons on to Aida (an embroidery cloth which comes in a variety of colours), you can work details and words in embroidery stitches, although other

Some delightful buttons in the shapes of prams inspired these new-baby cards, and the tiny toys completed the theme. These could also be used to make charming birthday cards for small children.

It may be difficult to believe, but the delightful trinket boxes shown opposite started

out life as containers for cheese similar to those below. A little creativity has

transformed them and concealed their humble origins.

BOXING CLEVER

Traditional French-cheese boxes are often made from plywood and are far too good to throw away. Decorated with buttons and braid, they take on a new lease of life and make charming little boxes to give as gifts, or to keep on your own dressing-table or chest-of-drawers.

Any selection of buttons can be used. If you have only a few buttons, the design can be worked as a simple decorative

motif or border, but the boxes do look especially attractive with their lids completely covered with an extravagant assortment of buttons.

Lightly sand the wood first, and then apply a coat of antique-pine varnish to deepen the colour. Glue braid around the side of the box to hide any writing before adding the button decoration.

Varnish will enrich and enhance the wood, but different effects can be

Empty cheese boxes in square or round shapes make ideal items for button decoration, and are just the right size to sit nicely on a dressing-table.

These

pretty trinket boxes

really look like

expensive shop-

bought items, but

couldn't be easier

to make.

achieved by painting the surfaces with acrylic paints. Cover with a primer such as white emulsion first, and then paint on the colour of your choice. Gold and silver are always attractive, and jet black can give the effect of Japanese lacquer. You could also try using decorative paint techniques such as marbling or faux verdigris and découpage around the side of an otherwise plain box.

Work out your design before gluing the buttons in place. Buttons with shank fittings will not sit easily on the top of the box while you do this, but some double-sided adhesive tape will keep them temporarily in place. Make sure that the surfaces are clean and free from dust to create

a good contact (you may also need to roughen the surfaces slightly with an emery board to create a key). Use a clear-drying strong adhesive when totally covering a box, overlapping the buttons and letting them support each other. Leave the box for at least 36 hours to ensure that the buttons are set firmly.

The lids have been

covered with

antique-pine

varnish to deepen

the colour, but you

could use acrylic

paints or even fabric

to cover the surfaces

before adding the

buttons.

Why not try mounting favourite photos in attractive frames

of your own design? Creative button decoration can turn even the simplest,

plainest frame into a work of art.

IT'S A FRAME-UP

Picture frames look very effective either highlighted with or entirely covered by buttons. These cheap frames have been completely transformed using simple button decoration.

Polished, mirror-finish gold buttons in bold geometric shapes give a striking modern look to the cheap frame on the far left. The buttons were placed around the frame and juggled about until the final design was decided on, and then glued in place. Use a strong glue – a clear-drying one is best, as any excess won't spoil the design. If the glue spills out through the holes in the buttons, carefully remove it when dry. Both surfaces should be clean and free of dust and grease to ensure a good contact. Test one button first, letting it dry completely for 36 hours. If it comes away from the frame with little force, you may need to roughen the surface of the frame slightly with an emery board to create a key for the glue before sticking on the other buttons.

The old-gold buttons and limed-pine frame in the centre look as if they were made for each other. The buttons had

shank fittings and were tricky to glue in place, so these were used to highlight the frame detail and positioned in the corners. One side of the shank was glued to the side of the frame.

Matt-gold highlights added extra interest to the shell, mother-of-pearl and pastel buttons covering the right-hand fabric frame. The buttons were sewn using a curved needle threaded with stranded embroidery cotton. Using three strands, secure the thread under a button, where it won't be seen. Take the needle up through a hole, across the button and down through the other hole, bringing it up through the fabric at the position of the next button. Continue sewing on the buttons, overlapping them so that the frame is completely covered. When you reach the end of the thread, make a secure knot and then conceal this with a button.

BUTTON PEOPLE

Make these charming little people by simply stringing
buttons together to form the bodies, arms
and legs. Add a small ball to create the head, and top it
with a button for a hat.

*These cheerful
button people will
brighten up any
corner of your
home. Make five or
six and turn them
into a mobile for a
child's room, or use
them as novel
decorative
ornaments for the
Christmas tree.*

String your chosen buttons on to
invisible nylon thread or matching
cotton. Use different sized buttons –
the smallest for the arms, medium-
sized ones for the legs and the largest for the body.
Buttons with shanks are ideal for the hands and feet,
or you could attach bells to add a jolly jingle. The
number of buttons required will obviously depend
on the sizes used.

Cut two lengths of thread, each of approximately
46 cm (18 in). Fold one length in half, and push one
end through a bell or the shank of a small button. Now
take one end of the thread through one hole of a medium
button and the other end of the same thread through the second

hole. Thread on several more buttons of the same size to form a leg. Make up the other leg in the same way.

Next, take both ends of thread from one leg, and push them both through one hole in a large button to start the body. Take the two threads from the other leg through the second hole of the button. String on as many buttons as required to complete the body.

When the body is the correct size, separate the threads on one side and take just one of the pair through one hole in the smallest buttons to make an arm. When this is the right length, take the thread through the shank of a button to make the hand, and then take it back up through the holes on the other side. Repeat this for the other arm.

You can now add a button to make a neck if required, or simply take all four ends of thread through a hole pierced centrally in a pressed cotton ball to make the head. Knot the thread tightly, as close to the head as possible, to secure it. Trim the thread and add a blob of glue to fix the knot. Tie coloured or invisible thread to another final button to hang up the button person, and glue this to the head to make a hat.

Give your button people individual characters by selecting buttons to suit – create a clown with bright primary colours, for example, or a jolly sailor in classic navy and white.

91

BOWS

PRACTICAL PROJECTS

CLASSIC CARDIGAN

Extra-wide patterned ribbon is ideal for enlivening plain knitted fabric to give it a new lease of life and a totally different look.

Transform a plain, long-line cardigan with ribbon to make a stylish addition to your wardrobe. You could either update a knit that you discarded long ago as boring and old-fashioned, or begin with a new one. Adding ribbon is the ideal way to smarten up a cheap, shop-bought jersey to make you really stand out in a crowd.

The look that you create will depend on your choice of ribbon. Use a wide ribbon with a distinctive *haute-couture* pattern such as the one shown here, and add it to the front and pockets of the cardigan. Begin by laying two strips centrally down both fronts, from the shoulder seams (allowing a little extra ribbon at the top for turning under later), and tuck the bottom ends neatly inside each front pocket.

To hold the ribbon ready for stitching, cut a piece of fusible interfacing to the same length and just under the width of the ribbon. Place the interfacing centrally under each strip and fuse it in place using an iron on a medium setting. Turn under the ribbon ends in

Strips of ribbon from shoulder to pocket, with ribbon on the pocket tops, completely transforms this basic cardigan.

line with the shoulder seams to neaten the top edges, and then hand sew down each side of the ribbon to secure it. Alternatively, work a loose zigzag stitch on a sewing machine. Take care when doing this, as knitting is such a flexible fabric that, if the stitches are too tight, they will snap or may pull the cardigan. Complete the decoration with a band of ribbon applique across the fronts of the pockets.

You could also add ribbon cuffs to your cardigan, or a simple band or bands of ribbon around each sleeve. To make a finishing touch, why not change the buttons too? As this type of ribbon is extra-wide, you can use it to make a set of matching covered buttons – follow the manufacturer's instructions for these, and then stitch them down the front of your cardigan in the usual way.

Make neat folds where the garment line changes direction, and turn under the raw ends of the ribbon at the top in line with the shoulder seams, and at the bottom to align with the hem edges.

You can give extra definition to the waistcoat with three pairs of diagonally folded loops of ribbon, evenly spaced on

UP FRONT

Use ribbon in a

pretty floral design,

with co-ordinating

buttons, to decorate

an uninteresting

waistcoat. You

could choose

stronger ribbon

colours for an even

more striking effect.

A simply styled waistcoat never goes out of fashion, and makes an indispensable addition to any wardrobe. A waistcoat is neat enough just to wear over a shirt, perhaps in combination with a smart tailored skirt or a pair of trousers, or can be slipped under a jacket or a heavy, blanket-type swirling cape for a "layered" fashion look that is also very warm!

A simple knitted waistcoat in a neutral colour can quickly be given a distinctive treatment with a softly patterned ribbon woven with a tiny floral design.

Starting at the shoulder seams, lay the ribbon down the front edges of the waistcoat as shown opposite, following the outline of the button wrap and pinning as you go.

either side of the button wrap. Fold and press each piece of ribbon to provide a pointed edge, and tuck the opposite ends under the vertical ribbons.

Hand sew all the ribbons in place with invisible stitches around the edges, being careful to let the knitted fabric move under the appliqué. The buttons on the waistcoat may now look out of place against the new arrangement, so swap them for pretty buttons which echo the floral feel of the ribbon, and you will be ready to go!

This type of ribbon decoration need not be restricted simply to waistcoats. A collarless jacket would also lend itself beautifully to this treatment, and you could even add a band of the same ribbon to a hat, and ribbon to shoes, to create a really spectacular "special-occasion" outfit.

Even when the waistcoat is worn under a jacket or coat, the ribbon will highlight its outline and provide a splash of colour.

SNAPPY DRESSER

What could be more appealing than this bright tartan waistcoat? It would give any plain outfit a lift, and

could be worn through the day as a casual accessory, or over a simple black dress during the evening to

provide a dramatic splash of colour. Add a matching bow tie to complete the look.

Choose a dressmaking pattern for a plain waistcoat, and cut out the two front sections from fusible interfacing. Cut out the front and back lining, and the back section, from fabric – you could select one of the ribbon colours, or stay with a more conventional black-satin lining.

Lay out the interfacing fronts, side by side, with the shiny (fusible) side upward. Take four tartan ribbons – three of 23 mm (⅞ in) in width and one of 75 mm (3 in) in width, and cut and place them at random over both fronts. Place the widest ribbon in position first, and then add the narrower ones haphazardly all round.

Adjust the ribbons until the arrangement looks good across both fronts, and pin to hold them in place. Carefully fuse the ribbons on to the interfacing, using an iron on a medium setting, and

This waistcoat with its front of bright tartan ribbons is very simple and quick to make.

then topstitch down the long edges of each.

To make up the waistcoat, first sew the front lining to each front section. Sew the front sections to the back, and then add the back lining to cover all raw edges. Finally, make buttonholes and sew on buttons.

To make a bow tie, cut a piece of fusible interfacing 36 cm (14 in) long by the width of the ribbon or ribbons. Fuse the ribbons on to the interfacing. With right sides facing, fold in the short ends to meet in the centre. Stitch the sides and turn the bow the right way out.

Repeat to make up a second bow piece.

For the strap, cut a 46 cm (18 in) length of ribbon. With wider ribbon, fold it in half lengthways, turn in the raw edges and topstitch all round; with narrower ribbon, cut and topstitch two lengths together, tucking in the raw ends. Lay out the strap, and place the two bows, right side outward, centrally on top of it. Bind the centre with a short strip of ribbon, and add a hook and eye to the ends of the strap to complete.

The white-spotted Swiss voile of the bodice on this
dress is decorated with diagonal lengths of floral ribbon.
Cut out the front and back bodice pieces from fusible interfacing,
using a simple dressmaking pattern if you wish.

Lay the pieces out flat, with the shiny side upward. Lay 13 mm
(½ in) wide embossed ribbons diagonally across the interfacing, with
the edges butting together. Pin and fuse the ribbons in place.
The ribbons are narrow, so there is no need to stitch them in
place, but make sure that you have pressed them firmly. Stitch
a fabric lining to the inside of the bodice.

Narrow

ribbon

embossed with

tiny flower

patterns is ideal

for a little girl's

party dress.

LITTLE
MISS PRETTY

Party dresses must be pretty and feminine, and adding ribbon

is the perfect way to enliven a plain dress or one that needs a

new look. This practical pinafore is very quick to make, and

slips over a dress to make a unique party outfit.

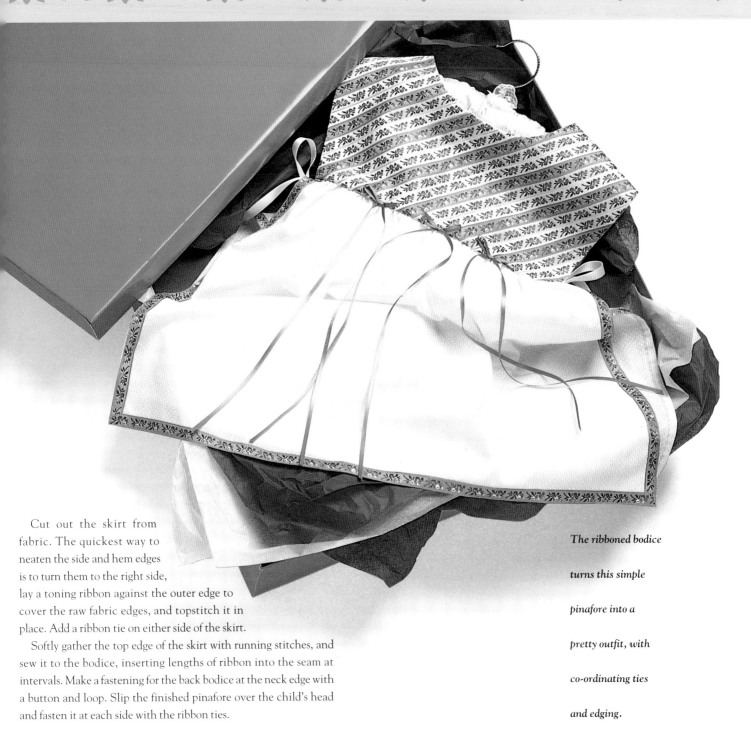

Cut out the skirt from fabric. The quickest way to neaten the side and hem edges is to turn them to the right side, lay a toning ribbon against the outer edge to cover the raw fabric edges, and topstitch it in place. Add a ribbon tie on either side of the skirt.

Softly gather the top edge of the skirt with running stitches, and sew it to the bodice, inserting lengths of ribbon into the seam at intervals. Make a fastening for the back bodice at the neck edge with a button and loop. Slip the finished pinafore over the child's head and fasten it at each side with the ribbon ties.

The ribboned bodice turns this simple pinafore into a pretty outfit, with co-ordinating ties and edging.

ONE STEP AHEAD

An elegant flower design in cream ribbon looks stunning on a black court shoe.

Put your best foot forward with these smart shoe trims. Plain shoes – whether destined for the beach or a party – look wonderful with the addition of ribbons and bows, while ribbon rosettes of all colours and sizes can be quickly made and anchored to the fronts of court shoes.

The contrast of cream against black creates the smart designer look on the left. Take seventeen 38 mm (1½ in) lengths of 32 mm (1¼ in) wide ribbon, and snip off the corners of each length to make a diamond shape. To form the petals, roll the long edges of the diamonds into the centre and secure each end with one or two tiny stitches.

Cut a 32 mm (1¼ in) diameter card circle, and glue the petals in place around the card.

Give espadrilles a new lease of life with pretty rosettes (below). You could add ribbon ties, too, as a special touch.

Glue a black button in the centre to complete the flower. Make up a second flower in the same way, and fasten the card circles to shoe clips.

Transform espadrilles into gala evening wear with ribbon rosettes (below). Use 75 mm (3 in) wide sheer ribbon in the colours of your choice, fold it in half and then gather it up with running stitch along one edge to make the rosette (see page 11). Bunch the rosettes

together across the fronts of the espadrilles, and sew in place. Finally, if you wish, sew two lengths of 21 mm (¾ in) wide satin-ribbon ties to either side of the backs of the espadrilles.

To make the folded-ribbon rosette above, cut twenty-one 75 mm (3 in) lengths of 15 mm (⅝ in) wide bordered ribbon, and a 32 mm (1¼ in) diameter circle of card. Fold and press each length of ribbon in half, and glue one length overlapping the next around the card with the raw edges in the centre.

When the rosette is complete, glue a gilt button in the centre. Make a second rosette in the same way, and fasten the card circles to shoe clips.

Gold-edged ribbon topped with a gilt button creates a sophisticated look for shoes (above). You could use bright ribbon and buttons for more casual daywear.

A simple but

striking ribbon

design decorates

this hair band.

HAIR RIBBONS

An elegant slide of

woven satin and

velvet ribbons

(above), and a

colourful rosette on

elastic (below).

Ribbons make ideal hair decorations. Instead of using them just to tie up pony tails and bunches, weave and create rosettes and clusters of gaily-coloured print and plain ribbons, and fix them to slides, bands and elastic straps for hair ornaments guaranteed to make every head turn in your direction.

To cover a plain slide such as the one shown above left, weave together narrow green satin and velvet ribbon. Cut four pieces of satin ribbon, each longer than the slide. Fasten them on the back, across one narrow end, and bring them round to the front. Secure the velvet ribbon at the back and start wrapping it round the slide. As you wrap, weave the satin ribbon under and over in a plain-weave formation. Secure the ends as at the start of the slide.

Double-sided print ribbon was used for the rosette on the left. Cut a 90 cm (36 in) length and turn under the cut ends, holding them with a zigzag stitch. Fold down one corner to make a point at one end. Sew a line of running stitch down the longer ribbon edge, catching down the folded corner. Gather up the ribbon tightly and fasten off

the thread. Coil the ribbon around the pointed end, sewing the layers as you work. Sew the rosette to elastic.

Mix three 2 mm (½ in) ribbons to form the plaited hair band shown on the left. Cut 230 cm (90 in) lengths of each colour, and glue them side by side on the band, starting about 10 mm (⅜ in) from one end. Wrap the ribbons around the band, keeping them flat, in the correct order and as close together as possible. Glue the ends inside the band 10 mm (⅜ in) from the end. To highlight the centre, make a flat plait the length of the band and tuck the ends into the bound ribbon, three from the end on each side. Glue in place.

To make the loopy slide below, cut five 61 cm (24 in) lengths of sheer ribbon: two print, two dark pink and one green. Sandwich the five ribbons together, and wire them to the slide to create eight loops. Spread the ribbons apart to create fullness, and wind a piece of ribbon around the centre to complete the "bow".

For the comb on the right, cut two 34 cm (13¼ in) lengths of 35 mm (1⅜ in) wide Jacquard ribbon. Fold each length into a loop and sew the cut ends together. Lay the two loops side by side, with the seams at centre back, and gather up the loops on either side of the centre. Trim with a sheer ribbon rose (see page 10) and sew on to a hair comb.

The "caterpillar" slide below is easy to make. Cut a sheer ribbon and a narrower Jacquard ribbon three times longer than the slide. Lay the narrower ribbon centrally over the wider ribbon. Turn under the raw ends and sew a running stitch up the centre through both ribbons. Pull up the thread to gather the ribbon down the length of the slide, and work a few stitches at the end to secure the gather. Glue the ribbons to the slide.

A double bow and ribbon rose decorate a hair comb (above); and sheer and Jacquard ribbons make an attractive slide (below).

Pastel-coloured ribbons create lavish loops on this hair slide.

BAGS OF FUN

Woven, sewn or glued ribbons turn plain bags into spectacular accessories.

Pick strong ribbons in hot primary colours, and use them to create fun bags for the beach or to carry home your shopping. You can make your smart, new-look carriers as small or as large and vibrant as you like!

To make the purse bag on the left, cut a piece of fabric to 34 x16 cm (13½ x 6¼ in). Fold 21 cm (8¼ in) across the width, with right sides together, and stitch each side. Turn the right way out to form the bag and flap. Cut five lengths of ribbon and stitch them along the flap. Make a handle from a folded ribbon, and stitch this on either side of the bag. Sew a piece of ribbon inside the flap, and a corresponding piece on the bag, to fasten the flap.

For the duffle bag opposite, cut a piece of strong fabric to 66 x 42 cm (26 x 16½ in) for the bag side. Choose three ribbons, cut each in half, and stitch them to each side of the fabric. Fold the fabric and join the side seam,

then cut a 20 cm (8 in) diameter fabric base and stitch this to the side piece. Turn the bag the right way out and bind the top edge. Stitch a casing below the ribbons at the top, leaving a gap on either side. Cut two lengths of 10 mm (⅜ in) wide ribbon and thread each through the casing. Knot the ends, and pull up the ribbons for ties.

To make the shopping bag, cut two pieces of woven tusible interfacing and backing fabric, each 32 x 45 cm (12½ x 17¼ in). Lay the interfacing flat, with the shiny side up. Weave ribbons over the interfacing and fuse in place. Fold with right sides together and, leaving the top open, stitch to the backing fabric. Turn the right way out, neaten the top edge and add ribbon handles.

PRETTY PURSES

Keep your small change or make-up in a pretty ribbon purse. Ribbon also makes an ideal decoration on tiny drawstring bags, for special evening purses. Match the ribbon colours to your favourite outfit, or make several bags for different occasions!

A simple criss-cross pattern looks attractive on this make-up purse.

Choose a plain-fabric background for this make-up purse. Cut out two pieces of fabric measuring 15 x 27 cm (6 x 10½ in). Topstitch ribbon diagonally in each direction across each piece. Turn under the seam allowance along the top edges, and sew each edge to one half of a zip. Stitch all round the remaining three sides, trim the edges and turn the purse to the right side through the zip.

The little bag on the right is very quick to make. Cut two pieces of fusible interfacing to 19 x 13 cm (7½ x 5 in). On each piece, lay patterned ribbons in bands across the shape, adding a plain extra-wide ribbon at the base. Stitch a casing made from a 38 mm (1½ in) wide ribbon to the right side, 50 mm (2 in) from the top.

Use a small plate as a template to round off the bottom edges on each piece, place the right sides together and

The "fabric" of

these little bags is

made entirely of

ribbons, with

tasselled cords to

pull them up.

stitch all round, leaving the top edge open. Turn under the top edge and stitch a narrow hem. Turn the bag the right way out. Thread cord through the casing and add a tassel to each end.

To make the bag on the left, cut a piece of fusible interfacing 38 x 30 cm (15 x 12 in). Lay it flat with the shiny side up. Lay 10 mm (⅜ in) wide patterned ribbons lengthways over the whole piece, and fuse in place. Fold the raw top edges to the outside, and bind with 23 mm (⅞ in) wide ribbon. Add a casing of the same ribbon on the right side of the fabric, 8 cm (3¼ in) from the top edge. Fold the fabric in half with the right sides together and seam. Cut an 11 cm (4¼ in) diameter circle of fabric and stitch this into the base. Thread cord through the casing and add a tassel to complete.

The beautiful woven cushion opposite is simple to make. Cut a 38 cm (15 in) square of fusible interfacing and lay it flat, with the shiny (fusible) side up. Use this as the base of the cushion cover. Use 15 mm (⅝ in) wide plain-coloured ribbons in pairs, and weave these with 23 mm (⅞ in) wide floral ribbons

CUSHION COMFORTS

Your ideas for cushion covers will be endless when you see the vast selection of ribbons from which to choose. The décor of a room will usually dictate the colour, but you can still pick your ribbons from many patterned and textured varieties. You could link a series of cushions, giving each one its own stamp with a different weave or ribbon arrangement.

Plain and floral

ribbons create a

lovely effect on the

cushion opposite.

See pages 12-13 for

examples of basic

weaves and

instructions.

to create the pattern shown here. When the design looks good and is tightly woven, fuse the ribbons in place using a medium-hot iron. To ensure that the ribbons will hold, turn over the interfacing and press it again on the wrong side.

The diagonally woven cover overleaf is made up in the same way as the first cushion, but the weave is different. Lay half

the ribbons diagonally across the interfacing, then tightly weave the remaining ribbons vertically over the interfacing. Fuse the ribbons in position, again pressing from both sides to achieve a firm fabric.

Overlapping diagonal ribbons make an attractive design on the cushion opposite (top). Cut a 38 cm (15 in) square of fusible interfacing and lay it flat, with the shiny side up. Use a combination of cream, rust and peach ribbons in 38 mm (1½ in), 32 mm (1¼ in) and 15 mm (⅝ in) widths to work the pattern. Lay the ribbons diagonally across the interfacing in both directions, as shown to create the design. Fuse the ribbons in place and, to hold them firmly, topstitch each one along the outer edges. Add definition to the central pattern with a border made with the rust-coloured ribbon. Pin this in position, and then topstitch the edges to hold the ribbon securely in place.

Toning ribbons

woven diagonally

create the eye-

catching design

shown on the left.

To create the diagonal design below, cut a 38 cm (15 in) square of fusible interfacing and lay it flat, with the shiny side up. Use 35 mm (1⅜ in) and 23 mm (⅞ in) wide ribbons in cream and rust, and mix these with a striped ribbon in rust, cream and green. Simply lay the ribbons side by side diagonally over the interfacing, and fuse them in place. Topstitch close to the edge of each ribbon to ensure that they are held firmly in place.

Make up each cover in the same way. Cut two back pieces from plain fabric, each measuring 38 x 20 cm (15 x 8 in). Seam the two back pieces together with a central zip. Undo the zip and pin the back to the front with right sides facing. Stitch all round, taking a 15 mm (⅝ in) seam allowance. Trim the seams. Turn the cover the right way out, and insert a cushion pad.

The ribbons used here were chosen to suit a colour scheme, but select your ribbons to match your own décor.

(Right) an elegant

pair of cushions

created with

striking designs in

rust, pink and

cream ribbons.

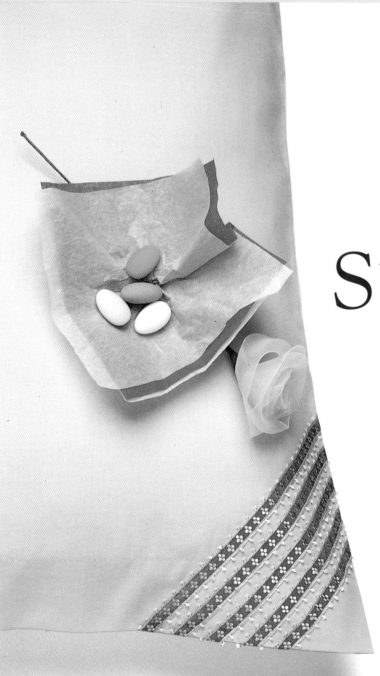

The ribbon decoration across the corner of the pillowcase on the left is simple but very attractive. Cut 10 mm (⅜ in) wide ribbon into five graduating lengths and topstitch them in place diagonally across one corner, leaving evenly spaced gaps between each

A simple ribbon design such as the one on the left transforms a plain pillowcase.

SWEET DREAMS

Plain bedlinen looks marvellous with motif additions, and pillowcases are the obvious target because they are quick to decorate. Match similar ribbon colours and pillowcases, and use pretty picot-edged ribbons to provide that distinctive touch.

ribbon and turning under the raw edges neatly. You could add more ribbon rows if you wish, but these may become awkward to sew as you move away from the open edge of the pillowcase, unless you sew them by hand rather than machine.

To create the design on this cream pillowcase, cut a length of picot-edged dark ribbon, to contrast with the background, and pin it to the open end of your pillowcase, 50 mm (2 in) from the edge. Stitch the ribbon in place. Next, cut a piece of narrower, cream-coloured ribbon into 36 cm (14 in) and 64 cm (25¼ in) lengths.

Beginning at the bottom of the pillowcase, position the 36 cm (14 in) length centrally over the wider ribbon, and stitch it in place for 10 cm (4 in). At the top, stitch the 64 cm (25¼ in) length of ribbon centrally over the wider ribbon for 34 cm (13¼ in). Tie the trailing ends of the ribbon into a bow, between the two sewn strips.

For the navy pillowcase, cut one length of decorative ribbon and pin this along the open end of a pillowcase, 10 cm (4 in) from the edge. Cut short lengths of the same ribbon and pin them diagonally from the pillowcase edge to the ribbon band, as shown. Tuck the inner raw ends under the ribbon band, and turn under the opposite ends in line with the pillowcase edge. Tack and then topstitch the ribbons in place to secure them firmly.

Ribbon tied in a bow gives a feminine look to a cream pillowcase (above), while a geometric pattern suits a navy background.

Towels of all sizes

can be enhanced

with ribbon

decoration.

A lace-ribbon

TRIMMED TOWELS

The pretty lace bow shown above is perfect for a small hand towel. Take a piece of 38 mm (1½ in) wide lace ribbon measuring the length of the towel plus about 20 cm (8 in) for the bow. Cut the ribbon into a short and a longer length. Turning under the raw ends, pin and stitch one piece along the woven border on the towel from the left-hand edge and the other piece from the right-hand edge, leaving 10 cm (4 in) of each ribbon unstitched. Tie these ends into a bow and catch with a few hand stitches to secure.

bow gives a pretty

finish to the powder-

blue hand towel

shown above.

Brighten up bathtime with beribboned towels. Pastel towels especially benefit from the addition of ornamental bands of ribbons. Use the ribbon shades to tie together an assortment of different-coloured towels into one attractive colour scheme to suit your décor.

For the zigzag design on the right, cut a length of 10 mm (⅜ in) wide picot-edged ribbon and fold it into a zigzag pattern along the woven border of the towel. Turn under the raw ends to neaten, and tack and topstitch in place.

To create the stripes below, cut a length of 10 mm (⅜ in) wide picot-edged ribbon in half lengthways, and tack one piece to each side of insertion lace. Stitch this in place along the woven towel border, turning under the raw ends to neaten.

For the "helter-skelter" design on the pink towel, wrap 10 mm (⅜ in) wide picot-edged ribbon around 35 mm (1⅜ in) wide lace ribbon to form a diagonal pattern. Stitch this in position. Stitch the ribbon along the woven border of the towel, turning under the raw ends to neaten them.

Ribbons are perfect

for co-ordinating

bathroom

accessories, as

this small set of

pastel towels shows.

Add sophistication

to your table with

smart ribbon-

trimmed napkins,

such as the one

shown below.

TASTEFUL
TABLE-LINEN

Plain ribbons look beautiful on smart table-linen. Make up a set of napkins with a table-cloth to match, or use your ingenuity to decorate the edges of each napkin with a different design. Weave the ribbons together at the corners or create a single striking motif – the choice is yours.

The possibilities for decorating napkins with ribbons are almost limitless. Shown on the left and opposite are two examples which are easy to make but look stunning. For the napkin on the left, cut and pin a length of 10 mm (⅜ in) wide picot-edged ribbon to fit along each side, 38 mm (1½ in) inside the outer edge. Pin a second length of ribbon 21 mm (¼ in) inside the first ribbon. Weave the ribbons together at the corners where they cross. Tack and topstitch the ribbons in place, stitching along both edges for a secure finish that will withstand laundering.

To make the design shown opposite, cut a length of 38 mm (1½ in) wide ribbon to fit along three sides of the napkin. Pin the ribbon in place, mitring the corners neatly and concealing the raw edges. Tack and then topstitch the ribbon, stitching along both edges.

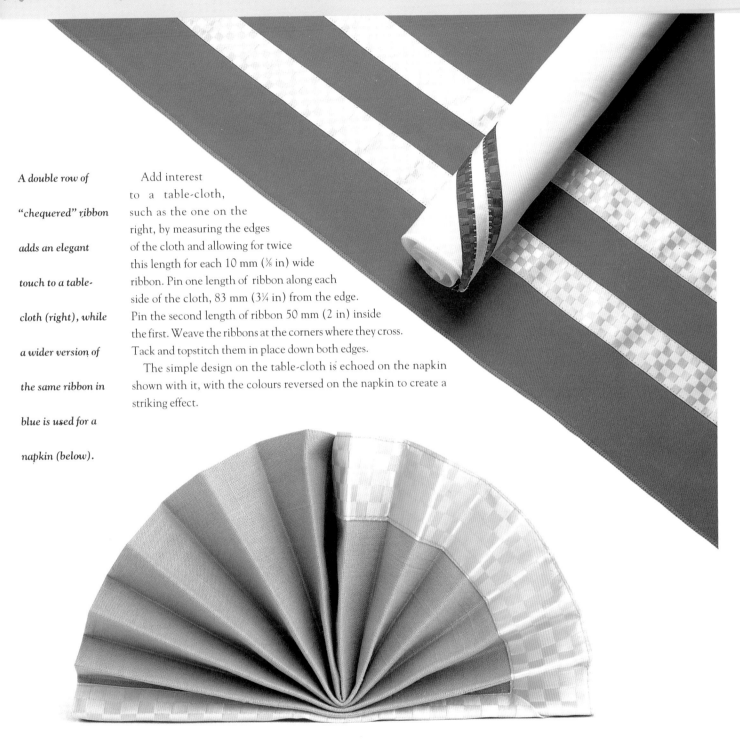

A double row of "chequered" ribbon adds an elegant touch to a table-cloth (right), while a wider version of the same ribbon in blue is used for a napkin (below).

Add interest to a table-cloth, such as the one on the right, by measuring the edges of the cloth and allowing for twice this length for each 10 mm (⅜ in) wide ribbon. Pin one length of ribbon along each side of the cloth, 83 mm (3¼ in) from the edge. Pin the second length of ribbon 50 mm (2 in) inside the first. Weave the ribbons at the corners where they cross. Tack and topstitch them in place down both edges.

The simple design on the table-cloth is echoed on the napkin shown with it, with the colours reversed on the napkin to create a striking effect.

The dainty bon-bonnière shown on the left would look attractive on any table. Cut a 28 cm (11 in) square of fine net and topstitch a narrow picot-edged ribbon around the outer edge. Place a few sugared almonds in the centre and tie up the net with two lengths of ribbon – one pink, one white – and into a bow. Trim the ribbon ends diagonally.

A pretty pink-and-white colour scheme has been used for the stunning display opposite.

Sugared almonds in a beribboned bon-bonnière (above) make a charming little present for wedding guests.

CHAMPAGNE RECEPTION

For the stunning table-cloth opposite, measure the table top and add 41 cm (16 in) to this diameter for an overhang. Cut a circle of plain white cotton fabric to this size. Neaten the edge and topstitch a length of narrow picot-edged ribbon around it.

Next, divide the cloth into six equal sections, and, at each of these points, work two rows of gathering stitches up to the table edge. Pull up the cloth and tie off the threads. Tie lengths of wire-edged ribbon into extravagant bows, and hand sew one over each gathered row.

Weave a magical spell around a wedding reception with beautiful ribbons. Combine embossed and sheer ribbons to make pretty candle holders, napkin rings and a ring cushion, and tie lavish bows to a ruched table-cloth to create a spectacular table setting.

To make the delicate ring cushion below, cut two pieces of white cotton fabric, each 23 cm (9 in) square. On the front piece, add a border of 38 mm (1½ in) wide embossed ribbon 15 mm (⅝ in) from the outer edge. Mitre the corners neatly to fit. Add a second border of 32 mm (1¼ in) wide embossed ribbon inside the first, this time overlapping the edges at the corners to form a neat edge. Topstitch both ribbons in place.

Gather up a sheer white-edged ribbon twice the length of the outer edge.

Spacing the gathers evenly, pin and tack this around the outer edge. With right sides facing, pin and stitch the back to the front, leaving an opening in one side. Trim and turn the cover the right way out, insert a pad and oversew the opening. Tie a bow of picot-edged ribbon at each corner, and a slightly larger one in the centre, to hold the rings, and sew them in place.

To make the unusual candle holder opposite, first cut a 15 cm (6 in) diameter circle of card, and stick a paper doily over the top. For the outer edge, cut 20 cm (8 in) lengths of white embossed 35 mm (1⅜ in) wide ribbon. Fold each length into a petal shape, and glue the petals around the ring in pairs, spacing them evenly. Glue two 20 cm (8 in) loops of extra-wide sheer ribbon in between each pair.

For the second layer, make up five large flowers from plain sheer ribbon. To do this, fold a long length of extra-wide sheer ribbon into petals, layering them one on top of the other to form the flower. Space the flowers evenly around the card and glue them in place, adding a large "pearl" in the centre of each. Leave the centre of the arrangement free for the candle holder of your choice.

This exquisite ring cushion (below left) has embossed-ribbon borders, ribbons at the centre and corners, and a sheer edging ribbon.

Make the matching napkin ring by stitching two 23 cm (9 in) lengths of 40 mm (1½ in) wide white embossed ribbon into rings. Place these back to back with a layer of interfacing in between, and topstitch them together around the outer edges. Form a white ribbon loop on each side and stitch them in place. Make up a sheer flower with a pearl centre, following the instructions given for the candle holder, and then hand sew the flower to the napkin ring to cover the joins.

The sheer cream ribbon used for this candle holder looks beautiful in the glow of the candle flame.

This delicate napkin ring (above) matches the candle holder beautifully to make a perfect table setting.

BOWS, BOWS, BOWS

Ribbon can be stiffened into shapes with specialist

solutions or a diluted PVA adhesive. Arrange the

ribbons, then simply paint over both sides with

the glue mixture. The ribbon will stiffen

and remain in the fixed

shapes, as well as gaining

a shiny surface that

creates an attractive effect.

Stiffened ribbon has

many uses – the frame

and plant pot on this

page are just two ideas.

se a coloured photograph mount as the
ase for the frame shown on the opposite
age. Cut a length of reversible green-and-
d gold-edged ribbon, and tie a bow in the
entre. Coat both sides of the ribbon with
luted adhesive, and then stick the bow to
e top of the mount. Stick the ribbon ends
either side of the frame
loops, using pins to
old them until they
e completely dry.

Woven plant pots
ok very attractive with
ribbon trim. To make
e design shown on
e left, allow for one-
nd-a-half times the
iameter of the pot top,
nd cut a piece of extra-
ide ribbon to this
ength. Fold it in half over the pot
dge and pin. Tie a large bow and sew this to
he basket, over the ribbon join. Coat both
he ribbon edge and the bow with diluted
dhesive and leave to dry.

The decoration on the cane wreath above
s simple but looks very effective. Bind round
he wreath with red-and-white gingham
ibbon, and fasten it at the top. Cut a length
of the same ribbon, tie this into a bow and
attach it to the top of the wreath. Cut the
ribbon ends diagonally, leaving them to
trail. Make a ribbon rose and fasten it over

Red-and-white

gingham ribbon tied

in an extravagant

bow and topped with

a rose gives this

wreath a lovely

country feel.

the bow. Paint the ribbons with diluted
adhesive and leave them to dry, and then
intertwine greenery or dried flowers
as you wish.

The little basket below uses the same
ribbon as the wreath. Bind the basket
handle, and tie lengths of ribbon into
bows on either side. Cut the ends
diagonally. Stiffen the ribbon with
diluted adhesive and leave it to
dry thoroughly.

The same gingham

ribbon transforms

the woven basket

below. A wide floral

ribbon would also

look pretty.

LAVENDER BOTTLES

Lavender bottles

woven with ribbons

make beautiful

little gifts.

Bottles of long-stemmed lavender, woven with ribbons, will scent

all your linen beautifully. Layer the bottles between the

sheets in your linen chest or airing cupboard, or

hang them in any position where

their delicate fragrance

will be appreciated.

Choose lavender with long stalks and
pick approximately fifteen stems, making sure
that they are all similar in thickness and length.
Harvest the lavender when it is ripe and in the
morning so that any dew will have dried.

Tie the lavender stalks together just under the heads, with
one end of a 200 cm (80 in) length of 3 mm (⅛ in) wide ribbon.
Bend the stalks back on themselves and fan them out round the
heads to create enough space for weaving the ribbon. Next, thread
the longer ribbon end on to a blunt tapestry needle, and use this to

weave the ribbon in and out, round and round the stalks. Weave to within a few centimetres (inches) of the stalk ends, and then tie the ribbon in a self-knot to fasten. Make sure that the stalks have been woven into an attractive bottle shape round the lavender heads.

To complete the bottle, tie a second length of ribbon around the stalk ends and into a bow. As an extra touch, cut one or two lengths of sheer ribbon in co-ordinating shades, and tie these into bows with the satin ribbon, leaving trailing ends. Decorate the bottle by sticking dried flowers into the ribbon bows, adding a blob of glue to secure. Make up several bottles in different-coloured ribbons, or keep to the same lavender colour to show what has been woven inside.

Use pretty pastel ribbons for the bottles, or a lavender colour to continue the theme. Tiny flowers tucked into ribbon bows add the final touch.

ACKNOWLEDGEMENTS

The Publisher would like to thank the following for their contributions to this book:

Brighton Bead Shop, Brighton, Sussex
Creative Beadcraft, Amersham, Bucks
Ells & Farrier, Beak Street, London
Janet Coles, Worcester

Janet Coles, Liz Gill, Deirdre Hawkin, Elise Mann, Jane Moody,
Lesley Stanfield, Jo Moody, Paula Pryke (flowers).

Button Treasures, Goswell Road, London

Susie Freeman, Helen Milosavljevich, Janet Slingsby, Lesley Tonge,
Laura Bangert, Clara Chan, Giulia Hetherington, Laura Wickenden,
Willoughby Werner.

Mokuba Co. Ltd., Tokyo, Japan
C.M. Offray & Son (USA)
Selectus Ltd, Stoke-on-Trent